ANALYZING CHILDREN'S LANGUAGE

Applied Language Studies
Edited by David Crystal and Keith Johnson

This new series aims to deal with key topics within the main branches of applied language studies – initially in the fields of foreign language teaching and learning, child language acquisition and clinical or remedial language studies. The series will provide students with a research perspective in a particular topic, at the same time containing an original slant which will make each volume a genuine contribution to the development of ideas in the subject.

Series List

Chomsky's Universal Grammar
An Introduction
V.J. Cook

The ELT Curriculum
Design, Innovation and Management
Ronald V. White

ANALYZING CHILDREN'S LANGUAGE

Methods and Theories

Tina Bennett-Kastor

Basil Blackwell

British Library Cataloguing in Publication Data

Bennett-Kastor, Tina
   Analyzing children's language: methods and
   theories.
   1. Children. Language skills. Acquisition
   I. Title
   401'.9

   ISBN 0–631–16374–3
   ISBN 0–631–16375–1 Pbk

Library of Congress Cataloging in Publication Data

Bennett-Kastor, Tina.
   Analyzing children's language: methods and theories/Tina
   Bennett-Kastor.
      p.   cm.
   Bibliography: p.
   Includes index.
   ISBN 0–631–16374–3
   ISBN 0–631–16375–1 (pbk.)
   1. Language acquisition – Research – Methodology.
   2. Children – Language – Research – Methodology. I. Title.
   P118.B46 1988
   401'.9–dc19

Typeset in 10 on 12pt. Ehrhardt
by Columns of Reading
Printed in Great Britain by
T.J. Press (Padstow) Ltd., Padstow, Cornwall

Contents

Preface   vii

Acknowledgements   ix

1 The Conceptual and Historical Background of Child Language Research   1

Learning the practice of the field   1
Theoretical discussion   7
Origins   8
Epistemology and pre-theory   9
Levels of investigation   11
Goals of CLR   12

2 The Stage of Theory Construction   13

General theoretical positions and methodological outcomes   13
The value and characteristics of theory   17
Development of theory   19
Theory-data interdependence   22

3 Naturalistic and Controlled Observation   26

Types of data sources   26
Reliability and validity of intuitions   27
Purpose and structure of experimental design   28
Difficulties of experimentally elicited data   29
Advantages of experimental methods   31
On replication   32
Types of experimentation in CLR   33
Steps in experimental research   34
Naturalistic settings and data   35
Available data   37
Dichotomy of progressive and conservative methods   38

4 Difficulties and Variables in Subject Selection   41

The function of the sample population   41
Subject variables   42

Number of subjects and its implications 42
Gender of subjects 46
Sibling position 47
Age of subjects 48
Other demographic and developmental variables 51

5 **Data Collection** 54

Disciplinary influences on data 54
Methods of recording 55
Diary studies 55
Other recording methods and their disadvantages 62
Advantages of videotaping 64
Frequency, duration, and longevity 67
On the nature of the observer in data collection 70
The research setting 73

6 **The Organization and Analysis of Data** 75

Transcription 75
Coding 77
Measurement in analysis 82
Types and functions of measurement 83
Ages and stages 84
MLU 85
Alternatives to MLU 87
Computer analysis 89
Reliability procedures 92
Statistical measurement 93
Interpretation 97

7 **The Practice of the Field of CLR** 102

Preliminary issues 102
CLR in the early seventies 104
CLR in the mid to late seventies 106
Recent practice of the field 108
Praxical clusters 110

Appendix 1 Data for chapter 7
Methods matrices 112

Appendix 2 Data for chapter 7
Praxical clusters 119

References 126

Index 147

Preface

This book has had a rather long gestation, almost literally. I began the research for what I thought was a much more modest project during the summer of 1984 in Oxford, England, while expecting my second child. The finishing touches were put to the typescript in the fall of 1987 while I awaited the birth of my third child. The project grew with me, in a sense. More importantly, it was the experience of watching the processes of language acquisition unfold in my own home which set me pondering over the adequacy of our research methods and theories. As I gathered published studies together and examined their procedures and conclusions, I felt some dismay at the clear lack of cohesion in the field. This led to a consideration of the field's origins and the reasons for its disunity which, though apparent to all its practitioners, was seldom discussed at any length.

As a field develops it inevitably outgrows its original goals, methods, and frameworks. In the past twenty years or so the field of child language research has grown rapidly, as indeed has the field of general linguistics to which it is sometimes allied. It became clear early on that learning theory was utterly inadequate to account for language acquisition, and the experimental methods often adopted by learning theorists turned out to be not entirely satisfactory either. On this point there is some debate. There are those who feel that experimental methods are best for producing a certain 'tension' in the field, out of which progress emerges, in the form of clearer goals, more specifically articulated hypotheses, innovative forms of instrumentation and other aspects of methodology, and, ultimately, explanatory theories. On the other hand there are those who will never be convinced that processes such as those underlying language and its acquisition can ever be clearly understood using artificially produced data, as it were. For these scholars, the point is to explain how language development occurs in each child given the vagaries and constraints of environment, genes, and linguistic structure, variables which cannot be successfully manipulated and still represent what they really are for the child.

Then, too, a sort of schism exists which centers on the goals of language acquisition research. Is the point to understand development in general by focusing on language in particular, or is it to understand language in general by focusing on its development in particular? The issue divides the field, sometimes, but not always, along disciplinary lines. For the linguist, the goal is almost always to understand language in general, and how grammar, considered virtually synonymous with language, emerges. For the psychologist, however, the goal is very often to reduce language to some other aspect of development, if the goal focuses on development at all. In addition, the notion 'language' has expanded over the years for some practitioners, so that it is no longer considered synonymous with grammar.

When the methods of experimental psychology were perceived as inadequate, and the methods common to general linguistics proved impossible to apply to children learning language, it became necessary to develop new ways to move toward the various goals which researchers had in mind. This in turn necessarily led to a re-examination of research goals. It is this process in which the field of child language research is currently involved, as manifested in increasingly detailed debates appearing in the literature concerning the shape of theory, critiques of methods, assessments of the significance of various findings, and so forth. These healthy signs of a vigorous discipline are to be encouraged even if they give the appearance to the field of a certain rancour, and make the disunity more apparent. I see them as growing pains which must necessarily be endured in the course of establishing child language research as a discipline in its own right.

Tina Bennett-Kastor
Wichita, Kansas

Acknowledgements

A number of persons and institutions provided tangible and less tangible support for the writing of this book. Certain aspects of data collection and analysis were undertaken through the partial support of a research award granted by Wichita State University (no. 3615–22) in 1985. Professors Orpha Duell of the College of Education, and Jim Klingsporn of the Social Science Research Laboratory at Wichita State University, were extremely helpful in matters of statistical analyses. Professor Klingsporn especially provided computer analysis relevant to chapter 7 and was responsible for the measure of redundancy which appears therein. Carl Castro, my graduate assistant for part of the project, helped to translate many published articles into categories of methodological variables, a tedious but essential process. He is now in the psychology program at the University of Colorado. Dr. Phillip Thomas, Dean of the Fairmount College of Liberal Arts and Sciences, has always been enormously supportive of my career. I am also grateful to the LAS office for providing the services of Fran Majors, who not only typed the manuscript but also caught several inconsistencies which might have caused more delays in publication. I wish to thank Ms. Majors for both her skills and her interest in the project, and the welcome diversions she provided in the form of discussions of Celtic music. Professor David Crystal was of greatest help through his brave reading of my wordy draft. His words of encouragement and constructive remarks were essential to helping me better define the audience and the most crucial issues which needed to be treated in the book. I also benefitted from some discussion of the project with Professors Paul Fletcher and Michael Garman at the University of Reading. I regret that I was unable to incorporate all their fine suggestions into the work. Finally, I would like to thank Wichita State University for granting me sabbatical leave for the 1987–8 academic year to allow me to complete the various tasks necessary for producing a finished book.

On a more personal note, my three children, Kristina, Patrick, and Liam, though distracting, are responsible for my continued fascination with issues in child language development. My husband, Frank Sullivan Kastor, has been enormously supportive in a number of ways: reading drafts, acting as a sounding board, providing sympathy and encouragement, and taking a rambunctious child or two out of my way when I needed to focus my energies on the project while on vacation in England and elsewhere. And I thank God that I was able to sustain the energy to complete the project before my return to teaching in the summer of 1988.

The most substantial influence on my life has come from my grandfather, Lee Edward Travis. His death on 9 October 1987 precluded his being able to see the book's publication. It is my hope that he might have been proud of his granddaughter's accomplishments. This book is dedicated *in memoriam* to him.

1 The Conceptual and Historical Background of Child Language Research

Learning the practice of the field

Few would claim that the field of child language research (CLR) is a unified one. No single theory dominates, and research practices are diverse as are the backgrounds of practitioners. It cannot be assumed that those in training for a career in CLR will necessarily receive rigorous instruction in the methods of research, and where such instruction is provided it cannot be assumed to be consistent across institutions. Often the graduate student is left merely to pick up methodology along the way, but since the sources which might inform one in this regard themselves represent considerable methodological variety, chances are that one's education will be eclectic, if not marginally coherent.

David McNeill once wrote that 'it is no one's fault' there is no specific methodology for the study of children in the first 18 months to three years of life. The rapidity with which language acquisition progresses 'constrains' the development of methods, and, consequently, 'the simplest measures – e.g., turning on a tape recorder – are as good as any' (McNeill 1970:6). If this were true then, it is no longer. Even prior to the early seventies scholars have been increasingly concerned with both methodological and theoretical, and even epistemological, issues in CLR. Furthermore, one can detect with approval a shift in the nature of these concerns as finer details of analysis have come to be the subject of critiques. Concomitantly, in actual analysis practitioners are attending with increasing awareness to alternative methods and their need for justification.

Among the earliest discussions, in 1960, Berko and Brown highlighted the disciplinary differences which have come to be characteristic of CLR practices (Bennett-Kastor 1986a). Focusing on design issues in experimentation intended to elicit 'errors' in the child's speech, or to determine aspects of language which were 'psychologically real' to the child, they noted that psychologists often wished linguists would take more care to describe their methods. At the same time, they appreciated linguists' attempts to extend research beyond support for one or another model of learning theory, models not well suited to language.

It would be easy, especially if one were to examine the early years of CLR, to conclude that it is a predominately experimental discipline. Indeed, since 1960, much ink has been spent on issues of experimental design. After the publication of *Aspects of the Theory of Syntax* in 1965, in which Chomsky made explicit the distinction between competence and performance, experimental methods were viewed as a means of tapping the child's competence and bypassing performance limitations. During the next ten years, CLR had a rather unified theory which began to influence methodology to a significant degree. Not only could experimental methods avoid the 'unsystematic' nature of longitudinal, uncontrolled observation, comprehension studies were specifically intended to bypass the question of whether gaps in production were significant.

The majoriy of methodological discussions in the years between 1960 and 1975 were undertaken by psychologists, whose training would have included research design. Linguists did not engage in as much CLR publication, and, although they no doubt shared a concern for appropriateness of methods, there were few forums in which these concerns could be expressed. As R. Brown wrote, it was only in the late fifties that the hybrid discipline of psycholinguistics emerged, and from the beginning it entailed the appropriation by psychologists of linguistics, rather than the reverse. Nevertheless, Brown considered linguistics to be the more 'compact' field; the diversity of psychology may in fact account for its great concern with methodology (1970: vii–viii).

CLR was of course never an exclusively experimental field, even in the hands of psychologists. In fact, its roots in naturalistic observation extend considerably farther back in time. William Stern, advocating diary studies in the early part of the century, contributed an enormous amount to the longitudinal base of CLR. He insisted that reliability and objectivity be paramount, along with a thorough knowledge of the nature of children (Stern, 1930: 37). Curiously, while many psychologists are responsible for the experimental studies in CLR and linguistics for many of the naturalistic ones, it was psychology – specifically child psychology – in which naturalistic methods originated.

Since the inauguration of the *Journal of Child Language* (*JCL*) in 1974, CLR practitioners from every field have had a ready source of methodological discussion, quite by design. At the International Conference on Language Acquisition in Florence in 1972, a formal resolution was passed to establish a journal devoted exclusively to child language studies, motivated by the scattering of materials, the adult orientation of work in journals of verbal behavior or psycholinguistics, and the non-linguistic orientation of journals in child development. *JCL* was to be 'the first journal . . . wholly devoted to the theoretical, methodological and empirical study of language development in children, and to provide a forum for reporting on and discussing current trends and events within the subject' (Crystal 1974a: i–ii). Especially in its 'Notes and Discussion' secton, readers could find a range of methodological issues, from questions of children's competence to make grammaticality judgments (deVilliers and deVilliers 1974), using 'talking dolls' to elicit such judgments (Lloyd and Donaldson 1976), and more recently, explication of methods to record everything a child says in a day (Wagner 1985), to theoretically and/or interpretively oriented discussions of the difference between 'overextension and underextension' (Kamhi 1982), and *a priori* versus *post priori* coding categories (Rispoli and Bloom 1985). While one could find critiques of published research in books and other journals, such as *Journal of Psycholinguistic Research*, *JCL* has been and remains the primary fountainhead. Its new editor hopes to maintain the data-oriented drive of *JCL* while also publishing more theoretical articles, especially for those areas in which a plenitude of data exists (Cruttenden 1986: 1).

As an illuminating example of the range of issues which is entailed by a methodological orientation – from theory and design to measurement and interpretation – one might consider the 'motherese' or input controversy which raged through *JCL*'s pages for a number of years, and rages still. While it would have been obvious to suggest early on that parental input accounts for acquisition, the immediate source of the controversy may have been Chomsky's comment about the inadequate data to which children are exposed (1965); hence, innate mechanisms must be largely responsible for the child's amazing feats of grammatical development (McTear 1978; Wells 1985). Brown (1973) made the claim that parental input frequency could not account for the order of acquisition of grammatical morphemes; Newport, Gleitman and Gleitman, publishing in the Snow and Ferguson (1977) volume, provided an explicit description of the syntactic and functional nature of mothers' speech to children and proceeded to examine correlationally the relationship between aspects of 'motherese' and child language growth. They concluded that differences in the child's linguistic environment might be responsible only for certain surface-structure features of language, processed through the child's own particular listening biases. Note from the beginning that the issue of 'motherese' and its facilitating effects (or non-effects) was in large part a response to a theoretical position – innateness (although Newport, Gleitman and Gleitman preferred to direct their focus away from this issue).

In *JCL* can be found a response to the Newport et al. study by Furrow, Nelson and Benedict (1979) in which the authors maintained that Newport et al. made unwarranted conclusions. The focus now was on the selection of statistical treatment of the data, the implicit assumptions in the previous analysis having been first that the effects of motherese would be uniform across time, and second that the child's age or stage did not influence change in the use of specific forms. Furrow et al. therefore matched the age and stage of the children in their study at the collection of the first sample so that any variation might be attributed to individual stylistic differences in the mothers rather than to differences in the children's language. Although Furrow et al. cautioned 'that interpretation of correlations is always speculative' (1979: 436), they claimed to have found four significant predictors of four measures of child language development – mean length of utterance (MLU), verbs per utterance, and, to a lesser degree, noun phrases per utterance and auxiliaries per verb phrase.

Barnes, Gutfreund, Satterly and Wells (1983), in *JCL* (see also Wells 1985), chose to focus on the question of what problems must be overcome if one wants to draw inferences regarding causal relationships between maternal speech and language acquisition. The subjects selected for the sample must first of all be heterogeneous and numerous; the speech samples must be representative in range, amount, and nature; variation in the use of the baby-talk or motherese register may be due to the addressee, therefore both age and linguistic development need to be controlled – a problem for which there is no simple solution; selection of the appropriate adult speech variables must be made, representing not just formal characteristics, but pragmatic, semantic, and discourse features as well; and, very important, some measure of the child's progress must be adopted. Usually, the measure has been a gain score (score at Time 2 less score at Time 1), but this is adequate only if the same scaling techniques are used at both times, which is difficult to do as child speech changes, and these are also subject to various sampling errors. Barnes et al. also pointed out that both percentage and crude gain scores are negatively correlated with, and therefore not independent of, scores at sampling Time 1. One solution has been the use of the residual gain score, which expresses the gain for a given subject as a deviation from the gain made by the sample. For each child, then, a difference score may be calculated between the Time 2 score which is predicted and that which is actually obtained (Barnes et al. 1983: 69).

Trying to follow their own advice, the authors proceeded to re-examine the relationship between the children's residual gain scores on eight measures of language use and six types of adult speech measures. Correlations were obtained between the proportional frequency of polar interrogatives, subject-auxiliary inversion and general semantic and syntactic development, and between intonation and auxiliary meanings and pragmatic functions. The authors assumed that such correlations suggested a probable causal relationship between linguistic environment and rate of language development; however, unidirectionality should not be assumed in an interactive situation such as mother–child conversation, and the absence of any clear account of how such effects are achieved requires the exercise of some reservation in the attribution of causality.

The motherese controversy continued with the appearance of an article by Gleitman, Newport and Gleitman in *JCL* in 1984 on 'The Current Status of the Motherese Hypothesis.' Conflicting results with their original 1977 study, particularly those attested by Furrow et al. in *JCL* (1979), led them to re-analyze their data. The central debate was characterized as concerning the extent to which effects of mothers' speech to children are broad and relatively straightforward (the position of Furrow et al.), or significantly modulated by the child's ability to store and manipulate input (the position of Newport et al. 1977). Because of the difficulty entailed in experimental manipulation of input speech, the relevant studies have been performed via correlational analyses, the problems of which are as follows:

1 measurement is of frequency of forms and/or content, although this may not be the important factor in language learning;
2 the non-linearity of learning curves – the more a child knows, the less rapidly his or her speech changes, and the mother may alter her speech accordingly – creates the potential for spurious correlations;
3 the direction of effect is a matter of interpretation.

Gleitman et al. used partial correlations (partialling out the effects of the child's initial age and language score for each measure) in order to try to remove the child's effects on the mother (more motherese would be directed to younger children, presumably) and the child's on the child (the younger the child, the faster the growth). Some variation in maternal usage and child language growth rate still remained, however.

Based on their objection to the perceived assumption that the effects of maternal speech would be the same over the wide range of ages and linguistic abilities represented by the Newport et al. 1977 study, Furrow et al. matched children at Time 1 for both age and MLU. However, while Furrow et al. found a large number of effects which Newport et al. did not, the utterance sample size was considerably smaller, and most of the variance they found was due to two of the seven subjects. Gleitman et al. suggested that many of the correlations found must surely be spurious – for example, mothers who used more copulas and contractions had children who used fewer noun phrases per utterance than other children.

Dividing their original sample into age-equated groups, each the size of Furrow et al's entire sample, Gleitman et al. performed simple and partial correlations for a number of measures, computed separately for each age group. Many significant, if peculiar, correlations appeared. The authors then performed split-half analyses (on odd versus even pages of the coding sheets) and took to be reliable only those correlations which were significant at approximately the same level as those for the overall data. None survived, and Gleitman et al. concluded that simple correlations are inappropriate for addressing the Motherese Hypothesis. Child age and/or linguistic ability – the child's initial state – remained a potential confounding factor of language growth. Partialling out the child's language score from each of the two age-equated groups, Gleitman et al. again performed overall and split-half correlations. Spurious results still occurred, such as a correlation of 0.99 between maternal unintelligbility and child verbs per utterance!

Gleitman et al. argued that Furrow et al. did not exercise enough caution in either design or interpretation. They maintained that if correlational data are to be taken as support of theory then they should

1 be consistent with what else is known about the phenomena of concern;
2 partial out known contaminants having to do with initial variance of the sample population;
3 be internally reliable, with the most conservative criteria for evaluating reliability;
4 be taken as '*pro tem*. and suggestive only, because of the enormous difficulty of interpreting them causally' (Gleitman et al. 1984: 65).

Gleitman et al. then reiterated their conclusions that the majority of the language-learning burden is carried not by input but, rather, by certain biases of the child language learner about both language and the handling of information (p. 77).

The next episode of the controversy was an article by Schwartz and Camarata on statistical issues in the relationship between input and acquisition (1985). They reiterated Barnes et al.'s (1983) points that gain scores are problematic because they are not independent of the child's initial status, so that something like residual gain scores are required to allow for comparison. The correlational procedures used have led to questions of the validity and interpretability of findings. The potential for chance significant effects is great wherever large numbers of comparisons are made, as is the potential for spurious effects due to intercorrelations within adult or child variables. Schwartz & Camarata reported that the probility of at least one spurious significant correlation appearing with such a large number of t-tests is 0.92.

Another problematic design issue Schwartz and Camarata noted is the degree to which one can make a clear *a priori* distinction between the independent and dependent variables, since no factor is being experimentally manipulated. Since the direction of influence may always be unclear, high intercorrelations, or no intercorrelations, remain difficult to interpret. Even the partial correlations used by Newport et al. will not insure that subjects are equivalent in linguistic ability; nor can one assume that the partialled-out measure is the one to which an adult is responding. Barnes et al. notwithstanding, heterogeneity of subjects is a problem in itself, since, although a researcher may control for initial level, there is no way to control for other differences throughout the comparison period.

Other problems in the design of input-acquisition research concern the reliability of measures and the probability of Type II or beta errors (i.e., failing to reject an unsupported null hypothesis); the assumption that frequency of maternal input is related to the child's frequency of usage, although other relationships are possible; the non-linearity of development itself, and of its relationship to input (curvilinear relationships may affect statistical results, as Gleitman et al. noted); and the atheoretical nature of 'shotgun' investigations in which the mechanism of influence is left unspecified. The sheer number of potential variables is problematic, and correct conclusions are not insured just because some variables are eliminated through deduction from a mechanism or theory, or through factor analysis. Since the goal of the research is to establish *causal* relationships, experimental manipulative design is preferable to passive observation.

Finally, Furrow and Nelson (1986) responded to Glietman et al. by, in effect, defending Furrow et al. (1979). Among other issues, Furrow and Nelson disclaim Gleitman et al.'s statement of the motherese hypothesis, note a 'confusion' of 'statistical significance with reliability' (Furrow and Nelson 1986: 167), and accuse Gleitman et al. of simply trying to support, rather than truly test, an *a priori* position.

This rather lengthy example of a controversy from the pages of *JCL* was intended to illuminate several points. First, the value of *JCL* once it began to be published is clear; major issues which may have originally been raised elsewhere find their way quickly into its pages. Second, one sees the breadth of the issues involved in the practice of CLR, issues of design and interpretation, of theory and even of pre-theoretical assumptions (e.g., that causality must be demonstrated). Finally, one can view, perhaps with frustration, the interrelationships of these issues. What began as a theoretically motivated proposition (input is inadequate; therefore, innate mechanisms are probable) rapidly filters down to the most minute levels of methodology – concerns with statistical measurement, for example. And at every point one is faced with a fundamental division in CLR (and in social science in general) between experimentalists and those who favor naturalistic observation (in general or for a specific study) and among interactionists, cognitivists, or 'autonomists'.

Theoretical discussion

Meanwhile, much literature has been generated in the realm of theory or even meta-theory, less so in CLR in the early years, but considerably so in general linguistics. While the practitioners of the field may have been primarily psychologists, it was linguistic theory that profoundly influenced method from the early days of the field's existence. We have already noted the strong experimental orientation in the mid-sixties and early seventies which can be attributed not just to the biases of many psychologists, but to deliberate attempts to put into practice the competence–performance distinction of generative grammar. Chomsky's notion that 'theory of a language' and 'grammar of a language' are synonymous (1957, chapter 6) manifested itself in an almost exclusive focus on grammatical (i.e., syntactic) development; the *Aspects* model further provided impetus for CLR in so far as an explanatorily adequate linguistic theory would have to meet similar conditions to the child's language-acquisition device (Chomsky 1965: 30–1). Although Chomsky himself remained silent on the appropriateness of experimental data, his defense of the validity of the linguistic intuitions of an individual speaker were taken as support for the (experimental) elicitation of children's grammaticality judgments.

While generativism was exerting its influence on CLR methods, there remained a contingent of practitioners who were not so swayed by the linguistic autonomy position. Followers of Piaget (the cognitivists) or of Vygotsky (the interactionists), for example, existed prior to the inauguration of the field of psycholinguistics, and continue to represent a viable force in CLR. However, the implications of these theories were profoundly different. First of al, they were more developmentally oriented; generativism was never intended to be. As a consequence, social and cognitive theories of language acquisition manifested themselves largely in longitudinal (hence naturalistic observation) or later in cross-sectional analyses from which development is inferred. While generativism was represented by methods in which concern for the structure of children's language was primary, social and cognitive theory were concerned largely with the functions of language and its relationships to other aspects of development. CLR in the European tradition was decidedly psychological; in the USA, it was becoming increasingly a sub-field of linguistics.

Origins

The dual and relative contributions of psychology and linguistics to CLR reflect the dual origins of the field which continue to effect its disunity to a great degree. Its oldest roots are in child psychology, itself originating in biology and medicine in the late nineteenth century. It is, in the late 1980s, more to be considered a 'stepchild' of two disciplines whose epistemological and methodological differences are yet to be resolved. The interdisciplinary flavor of CLR is not likely to be abandoned in the near future.

Perhaps the most profound characteristic of either parent field is diversity. Although R. Brown considered linguistics to be the 'more compact' discipline, it remains one of the few eligible for grants from the National Science Foundation, the National Endowment for the Humanities, and the Social Science Research Council, among others, which attests to the broad conception of language which linguists have typically entertained. Nevertheless, linguistics has traditionally been more closely akin to the humanities; witness the origins of the Linguistic Society of America in the Modern Language Association. As Lehmann described, the establishment of a separate organization resulted in many practitioners' forming 'closer ties in their methods and goals with social scientists than with their humanistic colleagues ... [yet] the Linguistic Society maintained its position with the American Council of Learned Societies rather than shift to the Social Science Research Council' (1987: 2).

Psychology boasts its own diversity, as attested by Brown (1970), and this is manifested as a dichotomy in developmental psychology specificaly between 'experimental' and so-called 'differential' orientations, according to Cronbach (1957). This clash, which has clearly carried out into CLR (albeit with fuzzier boundaries), is represented on the one hand by those who are sometimes associated with behaviorism and American psychology and on the other hand by those associated with Gestaltists and European psychology. The former experimentalists use controlled conditions to manipulate variables deliberately; they generally ignore individual subject differences, and they employ inferential, hypothesis-testing statistical models, the hypotheses themselves being generated by a theory, model, or set of principles. In contrast to this hypothetico-deductive, 'scientific' approach, differentialists are interested in the effects of variables as they actually occur; they focus upon individual differences; they tend to use correlational methods of analysis. (Compare the criticisms of Schwartz and Camarata with the work of Gleitman et al. or Furrow et al.) Further, because of the essentially descriptive nature of their studies, differentialists run aground with formal theory- or hypothesis-testing (Wohlwill 1973: 14–15).

Thus, CLR and child psychology share certain barriers to unity, illustrated as well in their respective searches for an appropriate disciplinary name. To call a field 'developmental' generally implies that age is the primary dependent variable; yet, since age is causally neutral and purely descriptive, and since children differ widely in their rates of development, the variable which cannot be controlled, one could argue that developmental studies must by nature be non-experimental. On the other hand, the prefix 'child,' as in 'child language,' suggests that the field involves the study of language as the child uses it, with no necessary focus on its development. A structural, cross-sectional approach is implied in this case, not excluding experimental analyses (cf. Wohlwill 1973: 13, whose discussion refers to behavior). The fact that CLR has no uniform name is thus significant of an ontological difficulty at its core.

Epistemology and pre-theory

Although psychology encompasses an array of sub-disciplines of great diversity, and linguistics is also becoming increasingly less unified as standard theory undergoes numerous revisions and counterattacks, one can neverthe-less detect general, pre-theoretical assumptions underlying each discipline which also create tensions for their stepchild, CLR. The assumptions of psychology are more often associated with those of social science in general, and those of linguistics with the humanities; yet this is complicated by the fact that linguistics, usually allied with the humanities in academic-political frameworks, is often considered by linguists to be a science, albeit one which does not fit the Kuhnian interpretation (Percival 1976; cf. Newmeyer 1986a;), and, specifically, a cognitive science (Chomsky 1957: 1965). Chomsky,

Table 1 Some contrasting assumptions of the Skinnerian and Chomskyan perspectives on language

Behaviorism 'science'	Generativism 'humanities'
1 Proper focus is verbal *behavior*	1 Proper focus is not behavior but the *competence* underlying behavior
2 Goal is *causal explanations*	2 Goal is discovering *universal* grammar ('linguistic universals'); mimic the child
3 Inherited characteristics include only the procedures and mechanisms for acquiring knowledge: elementary peripheral processing mechanisms	3 Human language requires a specific type of mental organization, different not just in degree, but in quality from other mechanisms for acquisition of knowledge
4 Knowledge mechanisms are generalizable across species	4 Language acquisition device is species-specific
5 Verbal behavior governed by inductively discovered abstraction achieved through reinforcement	5 Internalized grammar goes so far beyond primary linguistic data that it cannot in any way be an 'inductive generalization' from the data
6 Verbal behavior must be accepted 'in the crude form in which it is observed' (Skinner 1957: 13)	6 Linguistic intuitions must be invoked in order to overcome limitations of linguistic performance and access the underlying system (competence)

indeed, criticized the behavioral sciences for adopting mere surface features of natural science, thereby limiting matter to 'peripheral issues' (1972: xi). Considerable debate has occurred concerning the nature of science, social science, and the humanities, and whether these are, in fact, distinct categories which can be adequately defined. I wish to skirt these issues, however, and instead draw attention to what would represent two extremes of the social scientific and humanities orientations to language and the goals of a theory of language. For the former assumptions one can look to Skinner (1957), representing the empirical extreme, and for the latter to Chomsky's various works (especially 1965), representing (despite claims that linguistics is a cognitive science) the extreme of rationalism more closely associated with the humanities (see table 1).

These assumptions manifest themselves in different types of theories which in turn give rise to very different methodologies. Lois Bloom (1983: 844) has similarly summarized various 'tensions' in CLR which may divide researchers – specifically, tensions between language as autonomous and language as an aspect of general cognition (or, as Atkinson, 1982: 206, included, of social development), between mentalistic and sociolinguistic orientations concerning the relative contributions of the child and the social context of acquisition, and between descriptive and explanatory approaches.

For Bloom, it will be the task of the next generation of researchers to develop a theory which synthesizes these disparate elements. For Atkinson, the tasks are in particular not only the specification of general theories, but also the provision of 'reductive explanations' (i.e., more general explanations of development to which language development is reducible or by which it is accounted for), learnability conditions met in other areas besides just syntax, and the critical examination of theories of language development as psychological theories (1982: 234–5).

Levels of investigation

Regardless of the model one uses or its underlying assumptions, research in general typically proceeds according to six interdependent stages. These are (1) the construction of theory or at least some kind of explanatory framework; (2) the design of the research; (3) the collection and preservation of data; (4) the analysis of data; (5) measurement; and (6) interpretation of results, often in the context of the original motivating theory or framework. The theory, in turn, is also assessed against the results.

These six stages may be the focus of an individual's research simultaneously or consecutively. More often, theory construction becomes the concern of one group of practitioners while another concerns itself with the more data-oriented stages. Each stage, too, may involve a number of substages and require the resolution of interdependent problems. For example, at stages (2) and (3) one engages in the predominantely inductive processes of selecting a domain of inquiry (from which generalizations will be made). This affects one's conception of the kind of data which are accepted as admissible and consequently such decisions about collection and preservation as the appropriate means of recording, the number and nature of subjects, experimental versus naturalistic observation, and so on. An epistemological orientation towards social science might demand that the domain of inquiry be selected in such a way that a hypothesis deducible from a given theory may be tested; a different epistemology may demand that the data themselves determine the nature of inquiry or the patterns of analysis. But, as Furrow and Nelson emphasized, in neither case should pre-theoretical conceptions be allowed to be the judge of which 'empirically obtained results are "real"' (1986: 170).

The construction of hypotheses or theorems and their assessment is in effect an abductive process, where the application of a theorem to new data is deductive. All three forms of inquiry thus contribute to comprehensive research, although individual practitioners may have personal or academic biases. Kaplan (1984) has argued that all inquiry requires complementary approaches; to restrict investigations only to the so-called 'scientific' method is to rob them unnecessarily of their potential to attain truth. Whether or not CLR is a science is something of a non-issue, therefore. Not only do the sciences differ widely among themselves more than many people realize, the attempts to make a discipline 'scientific' often originate in a glorification of science based on the erroneous expectation that science has practical value. This is, however, to confuse science with technology, for today there remain major scienes with little or no practical application or its resulting technology: astronomy and paleontology, for instance. Our often false expectation that science will provide answers in turn constrains us into thinking that the appropriate questions are only those which we have learned how to answer (Judson 1984: 42–3).

Goals of CLR

Based on a reading of the literature, one can discern four goals of CLR. These are:

1 the confirmation of general linguistic principles;
2 the discovery of principles of the development of language;
3 the clarification of the relationship between language development and cognitive, social, or other forms of development;
4 the more or less atheoretical (if possible) description of the language of children.

Linguists may be primarily interested in the first one or two goals, and some will find them incompatible with the third (and fourth, as stated). Some psychologists may view the third goal as primary. One must ask whether these goals can be pursued simultaneously – certainly one must question whether they can be explored via the same methodologies. In the abstract, the goals are not necessarily mutually exclusive, but then research does not proceed on the abstract level.

Some of the challenges posed by the various stages and sub-stages of research, and the way their resolution reflects divisions in the field, will be discussed in subsequent chapters. It is clear that in assessing CLR, which is one of the purposes of this work, one cannot avoid the inherent disunity and its various sources – historical, epistemological, methodological. It is true that the field is genuinely interdisciplinary, but in itself this does not create diversity, since many interdisciplinary fields (e.g., neuropsychology or biochemistry) do not seem to exhibit the same degree of disunity. Although one senses that the gaps in the field between the two primary claiming disciplines are gradually narrowing despite completely different training, assumptions, and goals, and that someday CLR will align itself firmly with other human or cognitive sciences, practitioners for now must remain well grounded in the whole variety of methods from either discipline. In short, in CLR, there must be no 'linguistics' versus 'psychology' (Flores d'Arcais 1974: 328).

2 The Stage of Theory Construction

General theoretical positions and methodological outcomes

Clearly, the construction of theory is not a discrete level of research, but rather it affects and is affected by each subsequent stage and occurs as much as an end point as it does a starting point in the research process. Nevertheless, because in an ideal research world one's decisions at all points are guided by theoretical principles, it will here be treated as if it were an independent initial stage.

The fundamental assumption concerning theory which investigators accept is that no atheoretical research exists. Not only is it virtually impossible to complete a course of training in either linguistics or psychology without having been influenced by the major theoretical orientation of the graduate department, it is not possible to make decisions even about the number of subjects to utilize without betraying an epistemologico-theoretical bias. Since CLR is represented predominately by the two disciplines of psychology and linguistics, theoretically non-cohesive as these may be, its practitioners are prone to influences from both fields. In CLR there has been some theoretical merging, and the cognitive framework in psychology has also made the boundaries between psychology and linguistics difficult to discern. For purposes of discussion, however, it will be simpler to treat the two fields as if they were independent.

In psychology, the two major views of language have been the behaviorist and the cognitive. The former was dealt a seemingly lethal blow with Chomsky's 1959 review of Skinner's *Verbal Behavior* (1957), but since this was published in a linguistics journal, it actually had little immediate influence on psychology (Newmeyer 1986b: 52). Its followers are committed to the central idea that, like any behavior, language is learned and reinforced. Consequently, the child developing language need not be viewed as an agent acting upon conscious intentions; presumably, this would preclude coding categories based on such terms as illocution or intention (though not perlocution). In some strong versions of the theory, one would not even mention such concepts as 'mind' or 'consciousness', since these are not empirically verifiable. The theoretical assumption which directly affects analysis of data is that one can extrapolate from behavior in general the principles of linguistic and other behavior in particular.

Although in its most powerful form behaviorism is not a major influence in CLR, its more subtle variations are not wholly absent. Pea (1979), for example, accused Greenfield's adoption of information theory to explain early word choice of being simply a resurfacing of behaviorism, an accusation which Greenfield (1980) rejected with the statement that she believed it her 'scientific right and even . . . responsibility to develop this idea in the most fruitful way possible, unhampered by the constraints of past theory' (p. 221). Howe (1976), while not a behaviorist, revealed a decidedly empiricist bias when she criticized early classifications of the meanings of two-word utterances by scholars such as Bloom (1970, 1973), Brown (1973), Schlesinger (1971a), and Slobin (1970), arguing that justification for their categories of meaning has 'a shaky epistemological basis', assuming that children combine words in a manner similar to that of adults (Howe 1976: 40–1). Similarly, Francis (1979) challenged the evidence for functional categories of utterances. She suspected that Halliday's (1975) categories were ascribed largely on an intuitive basis; thus, his interpretive process would have been difficult to clarify and to assess (p. 204).

The cognitive or mentalistic view in psychology tends to minimize the role of learning or reinforcement in language development. In one form, the position holds that children have innate cognitive abilities, one of these being linguistic abilities (the influence of Chomsky on the development of cognitive psychology is here obvious; Newmeyer 1986b: 52). Alternatively, linguistic abilities may be seen to be 'overlaid' on more general cognitive faculties. Research reflecting this theoretical orientation would not be expected to emphasize individual differences among children, nor the caregiver's role in the child's developing language. The 'modular' variant of the mentalistic view considers that language is composed of numerous autonomous components for grammar, discourse constraints, belief systems, and so on. This view directly affects the first step of research – selection of domain of inquiry. Mentalistic approaches have tended in the past to focus on formal properties of grammatical systems and on the strategies employed by children (Prideaux 1985: 58–9).

Language and cognition have been viewed as related in one of three ways. The two may develop in parallel but independently, they may develop serially because language development is dependent upon cognitive development, or they may be related in such a way as to 'mutually inform and transform one another in the course of development' (Bloom, Lifter and Broughton 1985: 2). Research involving relationships such as those which may hold between Piagetian stages and vocabulary acquisition result from this general cognitive perspective (for example, Gopnik 1984), as do many studies in semantic development in the areas of overextensions and prototypical categorizations of concepts. This theoretical view demands accepted forms of measurement not just in language development, but often in cognitive abilities as well.

Another theoretical perspective often associated with psychology, but which may be represented in linguistics as well, is represented by the assumption that language development and social development – either as individuation or as socialization – are somehow associated. Research guided by such an orientation must necessarily focus on the social context of language development and especially in the relationship, linguistic or otherwise, between the child acquiring language and the persons with whom the child interacts, particularly the mother or other primary caregiver. In this view, also known as the interactionist position, there is no necessary expectation of universals in the developmental sequence (Wells 1985: 134), the role of individual differences and differences between groups is considerably more significant, and experimental approaches are virtually precluded (though one must keep in mind that at times given studies may offer interpretations consistent with several theoretical positions). Social development theory essentially derives from Vygotsky (1962).

Two difficulties with psychologically based theories of language development have existed. One is that, especially in the earlier years, the descriptions of the child's language which researchers from these schools proposed were not always up to the standards of linguists. In more recent years this problem has been less apparent. A second difficulty arose wherever language was assumed to develop out of an essentially non-linguistic conceptual system – the system does eventually become linguistic, but the mechanism by which this occurs has not been well described. Thus, for example, Dore (1979) has challenged Greenfield and Smith's (1976) claim that language and pre-linguistic gesture arise from the same cognitive source. Since 'language becomes autonomous and independent of conceptual development . . . linguistic structures must from the beginning be qualitatively different from other (action and perception based) cognitive products' (Dore 1979: 136).

The cognitive position in particular has been challenged by the problem that some linguistic concepts have little or no correlation with semantic concepts, e.g., grammatical gender; also, linguistic complexity – not just cognitive – would seem to determine in part rate of acquisition of structures (Schlesinger 1977: 154), although Block and Kessel (1980) found that it is the high commonality between syntactic and semantic complexity which is a predictor of acquisition order. Further, noted Schlesinger, categorization problems, which abound in language development and require that a child learn the boundaries of a concept, are heavily dependent upon the particular language one is acquiring (1977: 156).

In linguistics, the dominant theoretical position holds that the language component is autonomous; the implication for developmental study is that one can derive a fairly complete picture of language acquisition through analysis of the child's utterances, independent of (other aspects of) his or her cognitive development or social life. The position generally includes, moreover, innate ideas and principles activated by appropriate stimulation (i.e., input), which determine the form of acquired linguistic knowledge (Chomsky 1965: 48), the primacy of syntactic (structural) aspects of language which are assigned both semantic and phonetic interpretations (1972: 30), the impossibility of explaining acquisition by means of induction alone (1965: 33; 1972: 45), and thus the commitment that, concerning the role of data, semantics and situational context do not affect the manner (i.e., selection of hypotheses) in which syntax is acquired.

More specific characteristics of an acquisition model include

1 a technique for representing input signals;
2 a way of representing structural information about these signals;
3 some initial delimitation of the class of possible structural hypotheses;
4 a method for determining what each such hypothesis implies with respect to each sentence;
5 a method for selecting one of the infinitely many hypotheses that are compatible with the primary linguistic data and allowable by point 3

(Chomsky 1965: 30).

Difficulties with the interaction of linguistic theory and CLR are legion. First, linguistically based views have not adequately attended to the problem of development. Researchers have been inclined to describe successive stages of a child's grammar without positing mechanisms by which one stage develops into the next (but cf. Dore, Franklin, Miller and Ramer 1976, which attempts to describe transitional phenomena). Second, development of theory in CLR that is compatible with general linguistic theory depends heavily on the state and specificity of the currently reigning version of standard or other theories. While structuralism was dominant, experimental methods with their empirical flavor dominated the field. The earlier versions of transformational generative grammar seemed to command focus upon comprehension, in particular, of deviant and non-deviant sentences, given the primacy in the Chomskyan view of linguistic intuitions which were to be explained by explanatorily adequate linguistic theory. This, as noted previously, tended to produce much experimental research as well. However, in the seventies, as generative semantics and similar, non-syntactically based theories had grown in respectability, CLR became more likely than before to rely upon naturalistic observational methods of data collection. Lexical studies and semantic or case-grammar based categories become popular throughout the period. In fact, even when generative semantics had been given a proper burial in theoretical linguistics, semantically based approaches persisted in CLR (as, indeed, did alternatives to interpretivism in general linguistics). More recently, we have seen studies based on sometimes minute pieces of one version or another of standard theory and its rivals: Bloom, Tackeff and Lahey's (1984) research on complement constructions seemed to them to support the lexicalist rather than transformationalist hypothesis; Hyams (1984) countered that this interpretation was based on a misunderstanding of the transformationalist account of Koster and Kay (1982); Erreich, Valian and

Winzemer (1980) supported a transformationalist, hypothesis-testing account of the acquisition of syntax, and Nakayama (1987), using child data, presented a counter-argument to the Basic Operations Hypothesis.

The methodological problems associated with standard linguistic theory are also numerous. Many of these concern the problem of tapping linguistic competence, and will be discussed at more length in the next chapter. Primarily, however, the difficulties are in drawing the conclusion that a child's competence is somehow limited where other explanations are possible. For example, the particular cueing procedures used by the experimenter may constrain a child's response (Hart 1975), cognitive and experiential factors may play a role (Carr 1979), no theory of task-specific variability is available to aid us in determining the influence of the task itself (Fabian-Kraus and Ammon 1980), and the experiment may be an attempt to elicit a form which the child does not produce simply because he or she rarely needs it, as with complex subject noun phrases (Limber 1976).

MacWhinney (1983) has criticized the transformationalist position on the grounds that the subtlety of the aspects of grammar which demand an 'innateness' view requires elicitation techniques that are equally subtle; furthermore, there is an apparent stubbornness about some theorists in their refusal even to entertain alternative explanations, from pragmatic theory or principles of higher cognition, for example. Chomsky himself was aware of the very grave questions facing scholars attempting to construct an actual theory of language learning, although he relegated these to a footnote. These questions include 'the gradual development of an appropriate hypothesis', 'simplification of the techniques for finding a compatible hypothesis', 'continual accretion of linguistic skill and knowledge', and 'deepening of the analysis of language structure that may continue long after the basic form of the language has been mastered' (Chomsky 1965: 202, n. 19).

A second, more recent theoretical doctrine stemming primarily from linguistics is pragmatics. Originally associated with speech-act theory and the works of Austin, Grice, and Searle, it has come to be associated more with semantics than with grammar proper; it was also fueled by the generative semantics controversy and has persisted beyond its decline. One could argue that pragmatics is rightly a theory belonging to the realm of philosophy, but it has been so thoroughly appropriated by linguistics programs as a branch of study complementary (though not necessarily opposed) to generative grammar that it is probably safe to associate it with that discipline (Leech 1983 presented what he called this *complementarist* view).

The value and characteristics of theory

The narrowly 'scientific' study of child language is distinguished by its attempts at theory construction. It is often the case that, for better or worse (worse in the view of Deutsch 1983), scholars in the field tend to consider their contributions either primarily theoretical or primarily 'praxical' (Kaplan 1984: 9ff). Different types of reasoning are involved in each aspect. Whereas the practice of a discipline involves attention to ways in which a theory is relevant, and to methods, measurement, analysis, and evaluation, the theoretical aspect of a discipline treats the system being examined as an independent element, one in which the presence of a set of initial 'conditions' predicts the events in that system (Kaplan 1984: 82). However, not all theories are on equal footing as regards their predictive value. Where heuristic or progressive theories predict something new, it is possible to construct non-progressive theories which merely follow known facts (Kaplan 1984: 103); this has tended to be the part played by theorizing in CLR (Wode 1977). These theories are essentially descriptive rather than explanatory, because they consist of networks of so-called 'non-operating' definitions, i.e., they do not define variables appearing in testable propositions (Homans 1967: 11). They do not contain truly deductive propositions. Descriptive theories are common to the social sciences; still other fields, such as history, espouse no theories at all, but rather a wealth of empirical data and explanations which are not stated in propositional terms at all (Homans 1967: 29). Yet other theories are non-progressive because the sheer weight of appropriated 'facts' makes explanation impossible; this produced the demise of generative semantics in linguistics, for example (Newmeyer 1986b: 132–3).

In order to be truly explanatory, then, a theory must have predictive value, i.e., one is to be able to deduce 'empirical propositions from more general cases' (Homans 1967: 31), or what might be called 'first-order' facts from higher-order statements. An adequate theory is therefore constructed to have two characteristics: first, it must contain propositions that are sufficiently general that they handle a wide range of data, including data of various orders (linguists recognize the requirement as that of 'non-ad hoc explanations'); and second, the propositions must form a deductive system (Homans 1967: 31). Such theories have been constructed in other fields besides CLR; one might ask whether they can be merely appropriated. Often this is more difficult that one would wish, since it involves translation of key terms into the relevant linguistic domain. For instance, propositions in the behaviorist framework, such as 'the reward or reinforcement of a response increases the frequency or probability of its recurrence' would have to be altered so that the linguistic or conversational equivalents of 'reward' and 'response' are substituted. If this were accomplished, the proposition could presumably be tested against actual data.

Predictive propositions (theorems or hypotheses), essential to the testability of theory, are thus the point at which theory and data make contact. The more independent theorems which are confirmed by the data, the more the theory as a whole is strengthened. Given alternative theories, then, the theory is preferred which has more hypotheses that have been independently confirmed (Kaplan 1984: 110). Thus competing theories are not a situation to be despaired of, but a sign of a healthy and active discipline. By the same token, theories themselves are sometimes constructed theorem-by-theorem as evidence accumulates to support one notion and reject another, although there tend always to be data which are not considered valid (Kaplan 1984: 114). A non-progressive theory can therefore develop into a progressive one. The actual practice of a discipline hence determines the shape of theory in many ways – whether it must be retained, modified, or replaced altogether. In turn, a theory may lead one to look at old data in a new way, to perceive hitherto overlooked categories of data, and to otherwise re-organize and re-analyze data. (In such manner do many so-called 'creation scientists' re-interpret the findings of geologic studies that have been considered evidence for evolution.) Within language, a given theory differs from another in the variables it defines to be significant (in generative semantics, all 'facts' were given equal theoretical weight (Newmeyer 1986b: 133)); different theories will thus result in very different codings of data. Additionally, one must keep in mind that data are not always sophisticated concepts resulting from formal theory-testing – sometimes the best data for refutation of a theory are simply commonsense notions about the world (Kaplan 1984: 27) and various preconceptions.

Development of theory

Theories rarely, if ever, develop in their entirety in a short period of time. Usually one begins with what is known as a *theory sketch* or *framework*. This is an account which, though reasoned, consists of elements that are not strictly deduced, but rather connected only loosely or plausibly (Kaplan 1984: 19). A framework contains claims that are only vaguely stated and hence are not falsifiable (Perlmutter 1980: 196). Some of its statements may be proposi-tional and a few may even have predictive value, though most do not. Theory construction in CLR appears to be at this pre-theoretical level.

A framework or theory sketch represents an early articulation of ideas which are sometimes borrowed from neighboring fields and at other times begin as intuitive leaps or associations from quite unrelated domains. For example, Krashen's 'Monitor Model' of second-language acquisition was fueled in part by a book on tennis (personal communication). Frameworks may begin in analogy or metaphor, and even disproved theories can make useful metaphors for thinking about data (Kaplan 1984: 53), just as partially correct theories can be useful (Bloom 1984: 218). It should be clear that anyone concerned with theory construction must spend a certain amount of time unburdened by data and practice, in unstructured periods when assimilation, synthesis, leisurely reading, and the free association of ideas can flourish and perhaps give birth to insights that may later become important elements in a theory.

Requirements of a theory: general

Any theory in any realm must be empirically adequate. For Chomsky, a theory of language or grammar must meet the standards of descriptive adequacy by correctly describing the 'intrinsic competence of the idealized native speaker' (1965: 24). At least the theory must account for all the primary data: in linguistic terms, account for all the sentences and none of the non-sentences of a language (1957: 12). Atkinson believed that empirical adequacy had never been approached in CLR. Consequently, theory in this area must either be considered inadequate, or else judged by other, more formal criteria which will be discussed presently (Atkinson 1982: 1). In fact, theory in CLR is probably just immature.

Where, for Chomsky, descriptive adequacy in a theory was justified on external grounds and explanatory adequacy was internally justified, Kaplan (1984) discussed internal and external validation of theoretical concepts in somewhat different terms. Concepts are internally validated either by definitions within the theory or by their relations to other concepts in the same theory or sub-system being coded. The very concept of 'language' is validated in one way if we are discussing Navaho language or theories of natural language in general. Its validation depends on different criteria, however, in the sense of 'the language of music' or even 'animal languages' or, more relevant, 'pre-linguistic' communication. In contrast, one relies on criteria such as arbitrariness, learnability, or innateness for external means of validating the concept 'language' in a given theoretical domain. In a similar vein, an empirically adequate theory of child language development would consist of concepts which are empirically adequate both within the specific sub-system of (a given) child's language and within the theory or sub-system of language (phonology, lexicon, syntax, etc.) in general.

Requirements of a theory of language acquisition

Beyond the level of empirical adequacy and internal and external validity, a theory in CLR would in the ideal case involve also a theory of language, though Matthews (1983) expressed some pessimism about the relationship between language acquisition and linguistic theory. Where no adequate theory exists, there must exist at least a heuristic for a descriptive framework involving an examination of input data, a comparison of these data with the child's production, and a study of the phenomena in question as it appears in adult–child conversation, based on the 'best possible reconstruction of the adult model from the child's point of view' (Menn 1982: 134, 136). Only by delimiting the types of grammar which a child can acquire can the predictive value of child language theory be realized (Beckwith, Rispoli and Bloom 1984: 685).

Many of the problems that theory construction in CLR has faced by the requirement that it be consistent with linguistic theory have already been noted. We might also add that the child's competence can rarely be accounted for without access to meaning, which entails interpretation by the parent and/or researcher, and pre-syntactic and one-word utterances in particular have been difficult to explain using a formal grammatical approach (Atkinson 1982: 127–8). A theory of language development may fail if it cannot be reconciled with linguistic theory, but it is also the case that general linguistic theory must be reconcilable with child language data, including its variability (Local 1983). Difficulties which arise in CLR can similarly highlight previously unrealized problems within certain general linguistic frameworks.

The second requirement of a theory of language development is that it be consistent with theoretical principles in psychology. For some, the explanatory potential of general linguistic theory itself is grounded in its psychology of mental representations (Beckwith, Rispoli and Bloom 1984). The second requirement is essentially one for a 'reductive explanation', the alternatives to which are either teleological explanation (in which the properties of the goal or end point determine why structures appear in the order they do) and environmental explanation (in which output data are explained wholly by input) (Atkinson 1982: 20–2). Teleological explanation except occasionally in the guise of generativism, has not been of significance in CLR and environmental explanation is still being hotly debated (cf. the example in chapter 1).

Finally, a theory of language development must meet the requirements of a theory of development in general. Atkinson noted that most theories of development assume an increase in complexity or some other additive or incremental change over time (1982: 14–15). This implies continuity of explanation of the child's language at subsequent stages; any theory which proposed discontinuities would require substantial argument. Such was the demise of pivot-open grammar (Braine 1963), although it suffered from other shortcomings as well (Brown 1973: 90–5). The conditions which a theory of development must meet, then, are (1) that it explain the transition from one point or stage to the next on the basis of available data, and (2) that the subsequent stage be additively more complex than the prior (Atkinson 1982: 25–6). One way for these conditions to be met is by the positing of a sequence of theories, each of which characterizes the child's grammar at a given stage – an essentially descriptive procedure. One then proposes mechanisms – the explanatory component – to explain the transitions ('development') from one theory to the next (Atkinson 1982: 4–5). The requirements of a theory of language development thus cannot be fulfilled without the utilization of an adequate tool for measurement, about which much more is written in chapter 6.

Theory–data interdependence

Occasionally, one finds research which is not specifically intended to filter a particular theoretical position, but rather seeks only to perform a discovery procedure. Such research is often problematic in its usefulness, since the lack of an overt theoretical context may result in huge amounts of inadequately controlled variables. These in turn may easily lead to false positive or false negative findings (Kamhi 1985). One understands, in turn, the usual effects of theory on data in noting to what extremes researchers will sometimes go to explain seemingly erroneous data, or to adopt practices which suppress variable data which, if valid and reliable, would require dismissal or extensive modification of theory.

Data impose an adequacy requirement upon theory, and the scope of data might similarly constrain the scope of theory. Developmental data are collected cross-sectionally or longitudinally and represent distinct points in time. An investigator, in focusing on one such point and comparing it to adult data, would thereby severely limit theory much more than if one point were compared with a prior or subsequent point (Atkinson 1982: 3).

Residue data, which are unanalyzable because they do not fit the theoretical constructs, expectations, or techniques of the researcher, also influence theory, in particular when they become so significant in number that they may outweigh analyzable portions (Peters 1977: 560). When a large enough class of residue data accumulates, modification or dismissal of the technique, or of the micro- or macro-theory, inevitably ensues. Individual differences came to challenge generative views of language acquisition and doctrines of innateness, for example.

Homans has written that it is by the discovery task of a discipline that we determine whether it is a science, and it is according to its explanation task that we judge whether it is a successful one (1967: 7). Discovery leads to propositions which become the core of explanatory theory, thus discovery and explanation become inseparable from the point of view of the discipline as a whole. The relations articulated in propositions are organizational structures, in essence, which either emerge from or are often imposed upon raw data. It is the imposition of this organizational structure which reflects to the greatest degree the expectations of the researcher, and which has been most frequently discussed in CLR scholarship in the form of controversy over coding categories.

Among the preconceptions which have been challenged is the notion that the units and levels in child language are those of adult language (Howe 1976). Vihman et al. (1985), for example, took great pains to describe the operation of the category 'word' in their research with infants on the threshold of language. Another preconception concerning development is that it follows an orderly progression and is 'general' – i.e., all children follow more or less the same schedule. It has been assumed either by some that development, or, rather, acquisition, occurs 'across the board', or by others that it proceeds morpheme-by-morpheme in a type of 'lexical diffusion' phenomenon (Macken and Burton 1980a: 71–2; Snow et al. 1980). However, these are assumptions which must in fact still be validated, and generaly this means that a large number (N) and diversity of subjects must be considered. (In linguistics, large N can mean 'more than three').

Finally, linguistic data have been collected through the preconception that intelligibility is not a variable to consider and that unintelligibility – to be taken for granted – plays a small or non-existent role (Peters 1977: 560–1). This assumption persisted despite the analysis by some of so-called unintelligible data demonstrating its communicative value (as in (Ochs) Keenan and Klein 1975, Weir 1962, for example). Some assumptions underlie specific foci. In grammatical approaches, it was often assumed that child language could be investigated by more or less the same methods as adult language, or that distributional analysis, without recourse to meaning, was sufficient for demonstrating the existence of a category in the child's developing system (McNeill 1970:7). Later, in the sixties, transformational generative theory rejected the data of distributional analysis since they failed to tap underlying linguistic competence (pp. 8–9).

Data which are considered irrelevant by virtue of one's theoretical preconceptions about domain of inquiry may influence the very feature under study. Thus, had Scollon, intending a study in phonology, not included the utterances of the co-conversationalist in the transcript of the child's utterances, he would not have been led to posit two types of vertical constructions, one of which depended upon the intervention of the child's conversational partner (1979: 218).

The theoretical perspective of transformational-generative grammar, and all theories or frameworks which led researchers to examine only morpho-syntactic data, were in some ways limited in their demands on the scope of data. These were based on the developmental conception that children spoke an 'abbreviated form' of 'adult language', and resulted in constructs such as 'telegraphic speech' (Brown 1973), holophrastic speech (de Laguna 1927), or 'reduction transformation' (Bloom 1970) to explain the differential between obtained data and its presumed model (Ochs 1979: 17).

As theoretical perspective shifted and semantic regularity came to replace word-order regularity as a common focus, data were subject to interpretive analysis by which the child's meaning was inferred through a close attention to context (Bloom, Bitetti Capatides and Tackeff 1981: 403). This form of analysis allowed for the disambiguation of utterances, the sub-categorization of meaning relations into finer distinctions, and the identification of meanings with differing forms (p. 404). It solved a number of difficulties arising from limitations of surface-structure models – it was more inclusive, and did not artificially separate aspects of acquisition which turned out to be interdependent, such as grammatical development, language use, situational context, and the development of belief systems (Schieffelin 1979: 76). At the same time, it introduced its own brand of difficulties through the theoretical demand of empirical adequacy, among them development of precise criteria for using extra-linguistic information to aid in interpretation (Flores d'Arcais 1974; Howe 1976). In the semantic framework the distinction between linguistics and psychology has become particularly blurred, something that is problematic for those who insist on the strict autonomy of the linguistic component.

The major influencing factor of cognitive or interactionist frameworks upon data was the requirement of contextualization, which expanded beyond the notions of adjacent utterances and immediate behaviors to include cognitive development, individual differences, and so forth. This framework exerted its influence heavily throughout the mid to late seventies (Bloom, Bitetti Capatides and Tackeff 1981: 409), and continues to hold sway. Case-grammar and other semantically based approaches gave way to the so-called 'pragmatic' orientation which similarly demanded the contextualization of data. The following organizational structures of this framework directly affect data collection, preservation, analysis, and interpretation. First, children encode propositions in sequences of utterances and not always, as adults may do in a single utterance; second, the boundaries of propositional sequences can be assessed by examining eye gaze, intonation, pause length, overlap, and other paralinguistic features. These clues also help to determine the proper 'conversational units . . . relevant to . . . the issue of what constitutes a "turn" (Ochs 1979: 67). This imposed a requirement in data collection for visual context, and also aided in the solution of certain kinds of measurement problems involving the defining of the boundaries of 'units'.

Data collection and preservation in the pragmatic framework have led to discovery of the following developmental concepts, which are stated propositionally and hence become potential pieces of an explanatorily adequate (i.e., predictive) theory (Ochs 1979: :11–12):

1 the child becomes increasingly sensitive to the listener's perspective;
2 the child moves towards reliance on 'nonsituated' knowledge and away from reliance on immediate context;
3 the child becomes increasingly knowledgeable about the conventions required for successful speech acts.

In particular, the pragmatic framework affects data analysis through the restructuring of coding categories, as indeed do all frameworks or theories The particular name given to a group of data may be changed (e.g. 'noun' to 'labeling'), or contextual information may result in a given datum's being shifted to another category altogether, as when an apparent description (e.g., 'more juice') is seen from the context to be a request. The particular categories selected are often peculiar to a given framework – structural or functional or class categories. One of the most current trends, such as is illustrated by Wells (1985), is to practice theoretical eclecticism and use multiple coding categories (see chapter 6).

An adequate theory in CLR must, like any theory, be the simplest possible to account for the data. It must be consistent internally, non-ad hoc, descriptively adequate, and ultimately predictive. The major challenge to theory construction in the field comes from the necessity of explaining at least two phenomena – language and development, the traditional realms of linguists and child psychologists respectively – in such a way as to fulfill the objectives for each. It is reasonable to suppose therefore that some interaction of the various primary theoretical positions will be required for explanatory adequacy to be fulfilled.

One may sometimes imagine oneself to be theoretically neutral in focusing on a particular description of the child's language. Yet it is impossible to be free of preconceptions, whether these are explicitly stated as propositions or not. Preconceptions form a two-way path of influence towards theory and data, towards what we accept as solid theory, and towards what we deem appropriate data. It is therefore essential, as Jarvie reminded us (1970), to be both aware and critical of our particular preconceived notions and the epistemology they form.

3 Naturalistic and Controlled Observation

The somewhat artificial separation we have been making between the construction of theory and the design of research will here be continued, since the methodological outcomes of various theoretical positions have already been briefly noted. The aim of research design itself is the collection and analysis of valid and reliable data – a process which begins, specifically, with the design of observation. It is true that prior to this point a decision may have been made concerning the scope or topic of the investigation, and one might unnecessarily limit research design accordingly. For example, phonological development may be dependent not just upon characteristics of sounds themselves, but on the lexical items in which they appear (see Ferguson and Farwell 1975), or even the utterances and sequences of utterances in which they appear. On would therefore not want to assume that the larger context might be irrelevant.

Bloom (1974a) identified two issues in designing observation: the observation itself, and interpretation. The former includes the representation and preservation of data for analysis; the latter concerns how such preserved 'evidence' is structured (p. 83). It is the first issue, and whether to observe naturalistically or in a more tightly controlled manner, on which we will now focus (although a combination of approaches is also possible). Experimentation is of course actually 'controlled observation', but since the term 'observation' is typically used to refer to data collection in naturalistic settings, without interference (presumably) from the observer or other researcher, this convention will be followed here.

Types of data sources

Three sources of linguistic data are: indirect or anecdotal evidence; native speaker 'intuitions', especially as judgments of the acceptability of utterances; and 'raw' data actually manifested in conversational and other naturally occurring forms, usually preserved in phonetic or orthographic transcription (see also Prideaux 1985). About the first, there is little to recommend it. The scientific value of adult recollections is minimal, since the accounts generally cannot be validated. Even if the adult were capable of remembering with precision the thoughts, aspirations, and linguistic behavior characteristic of his or her own childhood, or that of offspring, these may not necessarily reflect the significant behavior of the child, but rather what the adult viewed as important in retrospect. Indeed, this may be why the behavior was observed and/or recalled in the first place (Bloom 1974a: 87; Stern 1930: 44). And yet, some anecdotal-type data have been of interest in CLR, especially in the form of interviews. Bretherton, McNew, Snyder and Bates (1983) summed certain aspects of children's communicative behaviors into scales and found significant interview-observation correlations for most scales (p. 309). Especially, they found that maternal interviews correlated as well as, or better than, observations with later child performance (although this was not the case for sociability variables). Garnica (1977) actually asked mothers why they adjusted their speech to their children; and Priestly (1980) pointed out that anecdotal evidence about children's pronunciations are commonplace and have been used to support competing theories about the significance of homonymy; interpretability is therefore a problem.

Certainly, one must question whether the second source of data is necessarily naturalistic or experimental, which introduces a problem of definition. While it is possible for judgments of acceptability to occur spontaneously in child speech, overwhelmingly these have been elicited. In naturalistic settings it happens that caregivers may expend efforts to get their children to say what they might not otherwise be inclined to – e.g., 'Patrick, what's this? What's this?' when Patrick's mother knows very well what the object is. Typically, when the elicitor is the caregiver, the data are assumed to be naturalistic, but where the elicitor is an investigator (who may be the parent as well), the data are considered experimental. In a world in which researchers often use their own children for subjects, it is difficult to determine the nature of data. One question which has not been addressed is the extent to which 'typical' caregivers actually engage in types of informal experimentation in their conversational exchanges with children.

Particularly, one must ask whether metalinguistic responses which are elicited can ever be reliable data about language development. The advantages and disadvantages of this data source have been well aired in the literature, and it is evident that they are usually assumed to be experimental data. For this reason, a discussion of the data of linguistic intuitions must also be concerned with the experimental method in general, and especially with the issues of comprehension studies, which usually are experimental.

Reliability and validity of intuitions

As they have played a role in general linguistic theory, intuitions typically meant the acceptability jugments of the linguist engaged in his or her own research, with the occasional 'polling' of whichever colleagues or students might have happened to be available on a given day – informants who could by no means be considered linguistically naive. Such a method must necessarily raise questions about its validity – the self-informant may have a theoretical bias which, inadvertently perhaps, selects the data about which judgments are made; or the bias may shape the judgments themselves (Prideaux 1985) and the degree to which the resultant data reflect reality. And, too, every linguist knows of the notorious instability of grammaticality judgments, a fact which undermines their reliability or consistency. These problems, coupled with the $N = 1$ (i.e., single and probably unrepresentative subject) problem spoken of by Prideaux, make the data of linguistic intuitions extremely questionable. Furthermore, the difficulties imposed penetrate through matters of research design, for the reliability and validity of data samples are judgments made from pre-theoretical notions, as noted by Kaplan, of 'the representative character of our entire range of experience' (1984: 107).

Upon this problematic foundation are built methods of eliciting the child's metalinguistic judgments. Some authors have insisted that these are simply unacceptable data; others, implicitly acknowledging their importance, have presented sometimes ingenious methods for tapping them. Still other scholars have been unwilling to dismiss such efforts altogether while at the same time articulating the numerous accompanying difficulties.

One might at first ask why a researcher should elicit a child's judgments, or why elicit a child's responses at all. We can briefly chronicle how time and changing methodological and theoretical perspectives have presented the answers to these questions. Although in 1970 McNeill claimed that no method for investigating comprehension yet existed, nevertheless such studies were performed, despite the assumption among researchers that comprehension preceded production and could therefore be inferred from it (Bloom 1974b: 295). These early studies, and most since the sixties, have typically utilized experimentation in which the child was expected to make some response to stimuli such as pictures, toys, commands, or other utterances. The experiments were designed to address the problem that, although features were sometimes excluded from a child's speech at the time of sampling, yet it was unclear whether this meant that the feature was not part of the child's competence. Experimentation began to play a major role in CLR primarily to tap comprehension, then competence; it is now no longer limited to these foci, however.

Purpose and structure of experimental design

Controlled observation is expected to yield causal information through the experimenter's manipulation of an independent variable (IV), information which cannot be provided definitively by observation alone (Wells 1985: 321). In experiments involving comprehension or judgment, the dependent variable (DV) has usually been the child's response to a stimulus (the IV) provided by the researcher. An example from the earlier days of CLR is found in Carol

Chomsky's (1969) study in which the IVs were the stimulus sentences 'make the doll easy/hard to see', issued to the child in the presence of a blindfolded doll. The child's response, to hide the doll or to remove the doll's blindfold, is the DV. When the response to 'make the doll hard to see' was that the child hid the doll, the researcher made a causal inference about how the child comprehends predicates such as 'easy/hard to see'. A change in the IV (e.g., 'make it hard for the doll to see') is expected to yield a change in the DV; when it does not, the researcher concludes that the child interprets both stimuli the same way.

Difficulties of experimentally elicited data

The structure of experimentation as so conceived is straightforward enough, but five general problems are associated with the data obtained through such methods.

1 One problem is illustrated whenever an experimenter must give the child commands to follow. Three possible outcomes may occur: (a) the child will respond as commanded, (b) the child will give some other response, or (c) the child will provide no response at all. In the first two cases, especially the second, the experimenter has no way of knowing on what basis the response was made (McNeill 1970: 13). In the third case, the experimenter does not know whether failure to respond indicates failure to comprehend. The first problem, then, is in determining the extent of the comprehension in such experiments.

2 The child's comprehension may in fact be 'multidetermined' (Bloom 1974b: 285). The child may base his or her response on something other than the IV. The particular strategies a child may use to respond might be completely obscure to the researcher, or they may simply be based on redundancies of context (p. 290). If the former, the problem may be generally stated as a lack of mutual understanding between child and researcher (Stern 1930: 43); if the latter, then the problem becomes one of how to design studies in which responses are geared to the linguistic material itself. Manipulation tasks have been found to introduce non-linguistic response biases, for example (Bernstein 1984), and Chomsky's 'easy/hard to see' task has been criticized by several researchers on the grounds that the task and other aspects of the context biased the results. For instance, using a screen instead of a blindfold condition, Morsbach and Steel found that children interpreted the predicates correctly more often (1976). Similarly, the child's responses may have been based on children's belief that they cannot be seen when their own eyes are covered.

3 Stern felt strongly that experimental data ought to be used only as supplements to, never substitutes for, the thorough observation of individual children. In this he was perhaps revealing a European bias of the early half of the century. His justification, however, brings up a third general problem.

Specifically, a young child can be distractible, losing interest quickly in the task, and has a tendency to tire (Stern 1930: 43). The younger the child, the more such tendencies are likely. This means that certain experimental procedures may wholly fail for certain age groups, particularly those including subjects who are on the threshold of linguistic communication, which many think is the most important age to investigate. In recent years, one of the controversies in the literature was fueled in part by the question of boredom or fatigue. Fremgen and Fay (1980) (responded to by Chapman and Thomson 1980) have argued that all overgeneralizations in comprehension are performance errors. Mervis and Canada (1983) counterposed that, in fact, many are the result of differential competence between adult and child; the major cause of the so-called 'performance' errors, they claimed, was task fatigue.

4 A somewhat related problem is that children do not always clearly signal their responses. They may laugh, smile, or shake their heads (Lloyd and Donaldson 1976: 412), or, as Brown discovered, respond with 'Pop goes the weasel'! One must then determine both the reason for the response and, more significantly, how to score it.

5 Finally, experimental studies are limited both by the researcher's assumptions about comprehension and by the situations which are provided for the children, situations in which obtained responses may or may not be the critical behaviors involved in comprehension (Bloom 1974a: 87). Presson (1982) found that, in a task requiring children to move two objects in relation to another where stimulus sentences were active, passive, cleft-subject, or cleft-object, the order of mention of the NPs became the primary strategy in comprehension, and not, as Huttenlocher and Weiner (1971) had concluded, grammatical function. This difficulty is sometimes hard to distinguish from the second problem in experimentation, since IVs are themselves an aspect of context. Pratt, Tummer and Bowry (1984), for example, discovered that children corrected errors in grammaticality of sentences more often when the error was morpheme deletion than when it was a word-order violation, and suggested that this was because the latter type is less likely to render the sentence meaningless. That is, they assumed that subjects' comprehension of grammaticality/ungrammaticality must be based on meaning rather than form, an assumption which may have also generated the two different IVs they used.

Despite the conspiracy of problems for the execution, analysis, and interpretation of experimental studies of comprehension, such studies continue to be undertaken, if not at quite the feverish rate as in the early years of CLR, and practitioners continue to suggest new methodologies or interpretations of previous studies. One or the other of two possible hypotheses appear to be the major themes for such studies. One, the transformationalist view, assumes that both production and comprehension are based on the same underlying competence but manifested in different 'performance modes', whereas the other view holds that two separate, different, but interdependent underlying processes influence one another to different degrees depending upon the developmental age and individual characteristics of the child (Bloom 1974b: 285–6).

The idea that competence underlies both speaking and understanding has certainly generated its share of experimental studies which are not strictly studies of comprehension but which share most of the previously discussed difficulties, in addition to posing some that are unique. Several researchers have concluded that there simply are no workable procedures for tapping competence in the early years, although children may be able to respond by the age of four or five by 'acting out' instructions such as those involving reversible actives and passives (de Villiers and de Villiers 1974: 17). There are serious questions as to whether or not judgments ought to be the criterion of competence and, if so, why there is differential transfer to various performance modes (Schaerlaekens 1973: 19–21;. It is clear that, where linguistic theory has influenced CLR, CLR has also demonstrated the inadequacies of aspects of linguistic theory.

Given the extraordinary methods to which one may have to resort in order to test the limits of children's language abilities (Ruder, Smith and Murai 1980: 202), and the other critical questions which arise concerning experimentation – for example, whether the goal of linguistic description is indeed to produce a grammar of competence; whether there are not certain contradictions imposed upon CLR by a framework which assumes underlying competence (Schaerlaekens 1973: 16–19); whether the data are generalizable to natural language use (Prideaux 1985: 9–10) – one must ask why the experimental method has been persistent in CLR, especially among psychologists (chapter 7; Bennett-Kastor 1986a).

Advantages of experimental methods

These problems notwithstanding, experimentation is indeed seen to have certain advantages. While some may criticize the limitations of experimental studies such as those in comprehension (Bloom 1984a: 87), others have seen these limitations as allowing the researcher a degree of necessary control over the diverse span of material to which a child must respond (de Villiers and de Villiers 1974: 14). Similarly, such methods may produce data which a practitioner would otherwise have to wait weeks or months for, if they appeared at all. Errors, for instance, are often viewed as evidence of a child's knowledge of regularity, but given that a researcher has an interest in a specific domain, there is no guarantee that the child during the sampling period will produce the sort of errors that the scholar can use for evidence. Experiments have thus been designed in which the child is 'forced' into making appropriate errors when asked to devise novel forms, make interpretations, or name unfamiliar referents (Berko and Brown 1960: 250).

Another advantage is that, when carefully designed to evoke what the researcher intends to test, experimental studies can be an important source of evidence for hypotheses based on reliable information from naturalistic studies (Wells 1985: 128), and can eliminate skewing of a sample that arises from unknown reasons in naturalistic date (Prideaux 1985: 9, 11–12). They can also answer specific, isolated questions with better control of contributory conditions (provided they are well designed), and the tasks can be repeated both as a means of comparison within groups, as in a before-after task, and across different age groups (Stern 1930: 39). Very important, too, is the replicability feature of experimentally generated data.

On replication

Replicability is essential in testing the validity and reliability of data. Tweney and Petretic (1981) (citing Lykken 1968) distinguished three types of replication. Literal replication is an exact replication of all procedures; operational replication is of only those procedures described in the report; and constructive replication, called by the authors the most useful type, is an attempt to imitate a study as well as to extend it by applying 'a new set of operational procedures or materials carried out in an independent setting' (p. 201). Cromer (1970), for example, took criticisms of Carol Chomsky (1969) into account when he undertook replication, and used stimulus sentences such as 'the wolf is hard to bite' and 'the duck is anxious to bite'. He was able in this way to confirm Chomsky's results while putting to rest some of the possible confounding variables in the earlier study (Aitchison 1983), although he was unable to anticipate many of the later criticisms which appeared.

Thus is replication significant, but fraught with challenges. So often, the procedures used in an experiment are not adequately described, so that one person's constructive replication may be another's complete failure to replicate, especially where results are not confirmed. Gleitman, Shipley and Smith (1978) thus criticized Petretic and Tweney's (1977) failure to replicate results of Shipley, Smith and Gleitman (1969) on the grounds that Petretic and Tweney had failed to use comparable subject groupings, coding categories, experimental procedures, or reliability controls. Where replication is the goal it is obvious that increased care must be taken in methodological matters. Sometimes, however, the original experiment may be ambiguously described. For example, the term 'repeated testing' has three senses: (1) demanding immediate second response to the same stimulus array and question; (2) presentation of immediately successive arrays with the same test question; or (3) recurrence of the same test question with either the same or a different array over the course of a test session, with other events or questions randomly intervening (Chapman and Thompson 1980). These authors pointed out that the third type is the most common sense of the term, and was what they used in an earlier study (Thomson and Chapman 1977), but Fremgen and Fay (1980), who got somewhat different results, assumed the first sense.

Types of experimentation in CLR

Though experimental research in CLR is strongly associated with comprehension studies (see chapter 7), it is occasionally utilized to explore production, as in the aforementioned work which forces a child into error making, and also to explore the relationship between comprehension and production. In the case of phonemes, children may be given pairs of nonsense words to repeat so that it may be determined whether they use certain distinctions interchangeably, or may be asked to distinguish referents of minimal pairs involving the sounds under consideration (Berko and Brown 1960: 527). Concerning production, experimental methods might similarly be utilized to test the conclusion by Fee and Ingram (1982), for example, that children who reduplicate do so to preserve the multi-syllabic character of lexical items which are beyond their production capabilities.

Lois Bloom has reviewed experimental approaches to the comprehension-production relationship and identified three general types of experimental tasks. One type involves manipulation of objects, pictures, or even the child's postures in response to the experimenter's requests, and the elicitation of descriptions by the child of object configurations. These especially have involved semantically reversible sentences. A second type entails a training task in which the investigator tries to teach explicitly a form, although, noted Bloom, training in understanding does not necessarily transfer to use, nor does training in use transfer to production. A third type is the elicited imitation task with the underlying assumption that, if the sentence given is too long for the child to hold in memory, the child will imitate what he or she thinks it means and thereby reveal comprehension (Bloom 1974b: 296–8).

There have been many variations on these three types of experimental tasks, and new tasks are still being proposed. Experimental methodology has never been perfected, however, and the same problems have continued to plague interpretation. One cannot know with certainty which variables of context have the most power in determining acquisition, and even what all the variables of context might be, given that they include the child's mental representation of the circumstances and events in which language is used (Bloom 1974: 302). Researchers turned originally to experimentation on the grounds that such variables might be better controlled, but this begs the question of their identification. Ideally, one knows the variables, and chooses to focus on a single IV, then to change the nature of the IV in order to observe the effects of the change on the DV, for it is only in this way that one can be sure which IV is exerting a causal influence on the DV. It is the assumption of causality in explanation that distinguishes experimentation as a method of the traditionally defined social sciences and defines the dichotomous nature of CLR, since linguists, most of whom receive little training in social science research methods, tend to use observational methods instead (Bennett-Kastor 1986a).

Steps in experimental research

In addition to the assumption of explanations of causality, experimental research is typically confined to standardized procedures which distinguish it from observational methodology (Prideaux 1985; and others). First, one formulates a hypothesis in a testable form by (a) defining the IV to be manipulated, (b) selecting the DV which will be a valid measure of the phenomenon of concern, and (c) articulating the prediction that change in the IV will effect changes in the DV. The formulation in this manner of sometimes both test hypotheses and null hypotheses (H_0) has given such research its 'scientific' character and reveals its usual dependence upon theory. The second step involves control of the variables, but, as noted, it has continued to be difficult to determine what all the variables might be, for example, in comprehension, so that one may maintain control. A third step which follows is the avoidance of co-variation of one or more variables with the IV, and yet it has become increasingly clear that co-variation may be a critical facilitator in acquisition (see chapter 6). When other variables are changing as well, however, it is not possible to identify clearly the source of change in the DV, which is the critical question. The fourth step, to which a separate chapter is devoted, is the selection of a sample of subjects who are (a) naive to the object of the experiment and (b) representative of a particular population. There has been a good deal of debate about whether this means that subjects in CLR ought to be homogeneous (in order to satisfy requirements of step three), or heterogenous, in order that causal variables in the individual characteristics of the subjects might be minimized when the group as a whole is considered.

A fifth step requires that the DV be guaranteed to be a valid measure. This may require an operational definition. For example, what might one mean by 'acquisition' of a construction? If a criterion is used such as 'the passive will be considered acquired when used x number of times', one must also decide how to score such responses as 'the horse was falled down'. The sixth step, or check, is to ensure that data are analyzable for a given hypothesis, i.e., make sure that the experiment tests what one intends to test. A corollary is to be sure that the hypothesis or the topic in general can be tested experimentally. Suppose, for example, one wanted to investigate the nature of marital disputes. It would be difficult, to say the least, to design an experiment which would yield appropriate data and still fulfill the requirement that subjects be naive.

For many practitioners, the notion of 'causality' in language is foolish, even if it were possible to identify, describe, and control all the relevant aspects of communicative context and all the features involved in facilitation of language acquisition. It is likely that major progress will be made only through the observation of naturally occurring language data, possibly subject to multi-variate analyses and various types of correlational studies, as Wells (1985), for example, has reported. For this purpose, the third source of linguistic data, so-called 'raw' data, is the best, although it is never really very 'raw'. Biere (1978) (as reviewed by Burmeister 1982), and others, have noted that the observer/investigator is engaged in an interpretive process which begins with collecting and categorizing data and extends through evaluation. Thus are even naturalistic data unavoidably subject to selection and manipulation at every stage of research.

Naturalistic settings and data

Problems

For every advantage of experimental data there is a complementary difficulty in naturalistic settings: multiple contexts (in many cases) with their uncontrolled, unidentified variables; the production of certain data left to chance and circumstance; skewing in data which may occur for various reasons – the subjects who agree to participate may be self-selected and non-representative (see chapter 4), the behaviors may be no more 'natural' than those evoked in experimentation, and the requirements of substantial duration, longevity, and/or frequency of recording may introduce seemingly intractable problems of logistics (see chapter 5). Furthermore, naturalistic studies are nearly impossible to replicate, and they cannot answer questions of causation (Wells 1985: 321).

Most of the problems, however, come under the heading of 'context', by which is generally meant all elements which either directly or indirectly affect the development of the child's language, elements as diverse as physical setting, behavioral and linguistic environment, cognitive and social processes, interactional variables, and assumptions both idiosyncratic and culture-bound. Some of these are accessible to researchers, but many are not (Ochs 1979: 1–4). To use naturalistic data requires, even more than in experimental research, that such variables be subject to definition and codification. Whereas both types of research must face the so-called 'two-body' problem in which there are three known sources of variance – speaker, listener, and the (statistical) interaction between the two (Dickson 1980: 123) – in naturalistic observation these must be semi-controlled not through standardization of linguistic material, but rather through measurement and situational variety (Goldman-Eisler 1972: 69).

Production studies have been more often associated with observation, and some have noted how the researcher is hindered by production data which are limited only to what the subject happens to say during the sampling period and its situations (Bloom 1974a: 87). It is never possible to know what the relationship is between the data obtained and the child's full production capabilities. Also, a persistent problem has been that practitioners often feel observation to be ill-suited to answering questions about children's comprehension of language. Ironically, experimental data have yielded as many difficulties even though they were collected to circumvent them.

Those committed to the explanation-by-cause requirement of theory and to deductive approaches often argue that observation must be defended where experimental studies need not be (Summerfield 1983, for example). And yet, Fassnacht (1982) pointed out that under normal conditions a discipline will begin with naturalistic observation and descriptivism, and only after having gathered all the relevant basic facts move on to more controlled observation. This, for example, was the direction in which the natural sciences moved. The experimental thrust in CLR, motivated primarily by psychologists in the field, may be subject to the criticism that it has been a premature leap, undertaken without the requisite history of naturalistic observation (Smith and Connolly 1972, cited in Fassnacht 1982). Social, economic, and political conditions which reward 'scientific' (i.e., deductive) methodologies may have contributed to this early emphasis on experimentation. However, over the course of the last fifteen years or so, CLR has turned increasingly to observation and has thus corrected its earlier imbalance. This has paralleled the entrance into the field of increasing numbers of persons trained in linguistics. Since then, a number of solutions to some of the difficulties of observation have been proposed. These will be briefly touched on here, but in the following chapters they will be articulated in more detail since they concern every stage of the research process. Basically, one sees generally a blending of methodologies which has enabled practitioners to take full advantage of both types of research design.

Advantages and solutions

Certain design procedures usually associated with experimentation, for example, have been proposed to aid circumvention of the two-body problem. Specifically, by repeated observations of the same pairs of subjects (usually mother–child dyads) in a variety of settings, it may be possible to assess individual 'scores' separately from those associated with the dyad as a unit, although the latter is also possible. This is a solution relative to measurement (Dickson 1980: 123–4), and it has been applied with varying degrees of success particularly to the 'motherese' body of observational studies. From anthropology has come the 'ethnographic' approach to observation. It has three advantages (Schieffelin 1979: 77). First, many different and complementary types of data are used, such as observations, interviews, recordings, and self-reports, across a wide variety of contexts, so that data are always contextualized; second, since the approach includes natural language, the resulting data are more integrated than 'piecemeal' experimental studies would yield; third, the approach is more flexible and responsive to the unexpected conditions that seem always to emerge in the course of data collection, and allows for continual reformulation and re-evaluation of questions and problems. Wells (1985) reported an extensive longitudinal study of over 250 children which represented all these advantages, for example.

Provided that the transcripts are adequately detailed, even the assumption that observation yields poor data for comprehension studies can be superseded. For instance, interruptions by the child may be evidence of sensitivity to grammatical boundaries, hesitation phenomena may signal difficulties, so-called 'repair' behavior or the presence of contingent queries may reveal linguistic competence through the child's abilities to reformulate, and gaps in the conversation may evidence places where the child knows that an element is missing though he or she cannot supply it linguistically (Ochs 1979: 70–1). To cite an example, Bloom, Rocissano and Hood (1976) used naturalistic data to re-test the notion that imitation precedes comprehension which in turn precedes production. They found that more utterances, and more utterances which were communicatively effective, were produced spontaneously by four children aged nineteen months to three years than utterances which were produced contingently upon the previous utterance.

Available data

A more creative approach to solving some of the problems of observation exists with the initiation of programs whereby researchers may share data. Although this may mean sharing problems as well, it will enable the researcher to perform studies without the numerous 'start-up' procedures which are often so time-consuming and fraught with difficulties.

Some of these programs are represented by collections of data in book form. Most people are familiar with the transcripts supplied in the Appendix of Bloom (1973). More recently, Fawcett and Perkins (1980) published the first four volumes of corpora for children aged 6, 8, 10, and 12, with 30 subjects in each age group, including two different situations. Fletcher (1985) also provides transcripts of a girl between 2½ and 4 years. One has, of course, no control over the form in which the data appear, but for many researchers this is a problem they will gladly accept so long as they don't have to go out and collect their own data.

An extremely promising and more controlled program of data exchange is CHILDES (the Child Language Data Exchange System), described by Macwhinney and Snow (1985). It enables researchers to conduct 'global' searches through data in the system, primarily (though not exclusively) naturalistic data. In 1985 the system already contained transcripts from fourteen well-known studies including those by Bloom, Bates et al., Brown, Ervin-Tripp, and Miller. The CHILDES Coding Committee has developed a proposed normalization scheme for all the transcripts, and all accepted data transcripts, or 'archives', are being reformatted to ensure consistency. In addition, CHILDES committees are continuing to develop various programs including those for searches, frequency data, MLU, concordances (key word indices), and others.

Systems such as these promise to be of methodological and theoretical value to CLR. In addition to providing a catalogue of the types of data available and standards for their collection, the developers hope to focus attention on issues in theory and method of transcription and coding, in the hopes that more rapid advances in methodology may be enhanced. On the theoretical level, CHILDES promises the ability to extend single-case studies to larger samples, including the empirical study of individual differences and the nature of input, increased access to 'rare events' which have eluded extensive analysis, the ability to compare experimental and spontaneous data, and increased possibilities for cross-linguistic analyses needed to clarify the issue of 'universals'.

Dichotomy of progressive and conservative methods

Inconsistencies which affect the reliability and validity of data, and which may enter into the research process at every stage, not only produce effects in the phenomena being examined, but also have ramifications beyond the single study in which they originated. Inconsistencies may render comparisons of studies virtually impossible, a problem which increases in gravity when cross-cultural, cross-linguistic comparisons are attempted. In addition, CLR is a field with high applicability to clinical and educational uses, through which inaccurage results have the potential to affect people's lives profoundly. Type-token ratios, for example, are frequently used as a measure of lexical diversity, and 'norms' have been established for these. Yet Richards (1987) pointed out that these ratios are highly subject to variation with sample size, and when number of utterances is standardized the ratio is shown to fall over time, leading to the impression that lexical diversity decreases as children get older.

For all of the above reasons, innovation may be suppressed. And yet, as Goldman-Eisler has noted, progress tends to spring from innovation in techniques, and in methods of inquiry which result from wholly new perspectives (1972: 70). The general conservatism of experimental method-ology, the importance of comparability of data collection and analysis, and the often frustrating delay in dissemination of new findings and techniques, all these nevertheless tend to impede progress in CLR.

Much of the conservatism in CLR would apparently stem from efforts to apply the deductive models of the sciences, models which require (1) pursuit of objective and controlled observation, (2) quantification, and (3) use of the experimental method for testing or suggesting hypotheses (Goldman-Eisler 1972: 68). These requirements led many practitioners, especially in the early years of CLR, to adopt the closest model that would fit (and in the methods of which many were already well trained) – that of experimental psychology. Where experimental research served to strengthen the position of child psychology within general psychology (Wohlwill 1973: 9), it may similarly have been viewed as a means of establishing CLR firmly among the ranks of social science.

Since, however, progress is more likely to occur where conservative trends are resisted, the entry of large numbers of linguists into the field must be welcomed. It is important to realize that 'comparability' of data does not necessarily preclude diversity. Data may be generally comparable and even complementary and still enhance progress. Characteristics of general comparability allowed Brown (1973) to use a fair amount of data from other research; complementary data allowed Wells (1985) to evaluate co-variance among the various types of data he had gathered. A synthesis of data such as that provided for by ethnomethodological approaches will guarantee general comparability as well as complementariness. Because these methods were developed for the purposes of anthropological-sociological observation, they are sensitive to the requirements of varying contexts and types of records, and are also capable of synthesizing the perspectives of observer and observed – i.e., the 'participant' – through the variety of records used. In this way, the investigator can solicit information about the significance of behaviors or events for insiders, in the framework of the larger familial, cultural, and social context. This information can then be used in the interpretation of the observational record (Schieffelin 1979: 76–7). The collection of data is thus always oriented toward the goals of analysis and interpretation.

In her discussion of possible approaches to observational studies, Bloom has made similar points about the 'etic-to-emic-to-etic' process which utilizes the subject's perspective as an analytical *a priori* framework through which data from a larger group of subjects (now with a pre-selected observer's – i.e. etic – point of view) can be examined (1974a: 87; see also Pike 1967).

The successful utilization of ethnomethodological procedures requires four types of accounts (see Schieffelin 1979), including:

1 records concerning how the recurrent and significant activities of the subjects are organized (ie.g., bedtime routines, family meals, child care procedures, and so on);
2 notes, generally in diary form, on general characteristics of the children's health and development, as well as other factors which might affect these, such as the birth of a sibling, loss of a family member, change of household, and so forth;
3 interviews with significant adult figures concerning the cultural or familial belief system regarding social, intellectual, communicative, emotional, and physical development (e.g., the value of independence for young children, the family's attitudes towards talk, beliefs about male/ female differences in abilities and preferences, and so on);

4 naturalistic, longitudinal speech sampling (enhanced if possible by cross-
   sectional studies of large numbers of subjects), supplemented by detailed
   contextual records, which focus on a subset of children in the group.

At least some of these records ought to be supplemented with diaries kept by
the primary caregivers, as this will help to ensure a balance of records from
both participants' and observers' perspectives.

4 Difficulties and Variables in Subject Selection

The function of the sample population

Subjects for research who are carefully selected and whose characteristics are well described provide investigators with three potential benefits. First, one can learn the degree to which the subjects of a given study match those in other research, which aids in the evaluation process. Second, the thorough description of subjects enhances replication. Finally, the theorist may be able to infer possible variables which are critical in shaping the form of language development (Wickstrom, Goldstein and Johnson 1985: 282, discussing the description of subjects in language disorders literature).

If our purposes in CLR include making quantifiable comparisons among studies, then in an ideal world each researcher will obtain as large an amount of data as possible from as many children as possible (Stern 1930: 46), who either represent a wide range of backgrounds, or who are homogeneous. If on the other hand one of the purposes of CLR is to understand the extent to which language development is either shaped by, or itself shapes, the personality, sub-culture, and intelligence of an individual child, then the ideal investigator will methodically examine each detail of all the potentially influential characteristics of individual children. This represents but one dichotomy in research design, one concerning amount of data and nature and number of subjects. It is in the choice of subjects that, perhaps, one sees most clearly epistemological contrasts between the contributing disciplines in CLR – the generalizability of the individual's experience on the one hand, and the necessity of smoothing over individual variation for the demands of so-called normal distributions. These views are not entirely unresolvable, for no matter how many subjects one has they can always be encountered individually.

More often than one might desire, however, subject selection is made on the basis of accidental factors. Questions of accessibility of subjects, complexity of the analysis, and even longevity of the research period may produce research 'default' (versus 'design'). It is also true that multiple interactions among subject variables conspire to make it impossible for the researcher to select subjects freely. These, in combination with demands of specific research practices such as measurement techniques, all contribute to the immense difficulties involved in the selection of a sample population.

Subject variables

Subject variables are defined as inherent characteristics of subjects (Wright 1976: 43). Because they frequently cannot be manipulated (except through selection), some often become IVs in the research design. But since they may also be DVs, it is impossible to discuss subject variables independently of measurement, a topic reserved for detailed discussion in the next chapter. As an example, one might imagine that a subject's linguistic ability itself is a variable. It might be a means of measurement (MLU, type-token ratio, and so forth), it might be the basis for classification of subjects into comparison groups (IV), it might be one of the DVs as measured against, say, maternal input; and it might certainly be confounded with numerous other subject variables, all of which present the same array of possibilities.

Number of subjects and its implications

Certainly one of the most significant decisions a researcher makes concerns the number of subjects. It is easiest to find praise for large numbers and disparaging remarks about small N. Tversky and Kahnemann (1971) accused psychologists (although they might have been addressing linguists) of favoring 'The Law of Small Numbers' – gross overconfidence in small N. Sample sizes which are too small, either because N is small or because the number of utterances from each subject is, may be problematic if the analysis is self-contradictory, counter-intuitive, or contradictory of other studies. Particularly where one is concerned with a specific feature of communicative competence, small N may result in fewer possibilities for that feature's emergence in the corpus. Obviously, one could make a much stronger case if evidence occurred with greater frequency, and were supported by other aspects of development and a large number of subjects (Bloom, Bitetti Capatides and Tackeff 1981: 404).

Since, as sample size decreases, it is necessary to obtain larger and larger differences among subjects before statistical significance can be reached, the social sciences in particular have tended to pursue large samples. How large a sample should be is of course an arguable point – the answer depends upon the nature of the distribution of the relevant variable, yet this is usually what one is trying to find out (Woods, Fletcher and Hughes 1986: 103). The answer also depends upon the independence of observations, a question which itself is unanswerable for many types of linguistic data (pp. 103–4).

One might gather from the preceding that large N is the only justifiable choice to make, but this is not the case. In fact, large samples also have their problems, and criticisms of them have appeared in the literature as well. It is helpful to look at the advantages and disadvantages that have been associated with various sample sizes, either small (between one and five) or large (over thirty).

Small N studies

Small N studies are rather profuse in CLR as well as other fields. Fletcher pointed out that small numbers of subjects are often necessitated by frequent sampling and the time required to transcribe and analyze data – practices which make large N unwieldy (1985: 10). In the behavioral sciences, the study of individual subjects has a long history. In communicative disorders, single-subject strategies have been appealing; this field even has a full-length book devoted to the topic (McReynolds and Kearns 1983). Such research has been justified as being the only appropriate way of gaining understanding of the behavior of individuals over and against the study of statistical norms. This view is especially strong where applied or clinical research is concerned, since clinical populations are dealt with individual by individual (Siegel and Young 1987: 194).

The objections to large N which have been raised particularly in the applied fields are that

1 it is difficult to bridge the gap between science and practice;
2 measures of central tendency may not fit any single individual;
3 a large pool of homogeneous subjects is difficult to obtain, may delay the onset of research, and may not match subjects with whom clinicians work;
4 large N studies are less flexible than those using single subjects and so are less like the actual clinical or applied course of events;
5 the clinical significance of findings is not captured by statistical significance, since this may occur in the absence of either theoretical or practical utility, whereas single-subject research is focused on real behavioral results (Siegel and Young 1987: 196).

At least one author felt that in studies with large N, especially multi-variate studies, the measures used are often not sensitive enough to differentiate relationships of the complexity typical in language-related behaviors (Kamhi 1985: 288–90). Another frequent shortcoming is an unacknowledged or weak 'theoretical context', in which the investigator is searching for anything at all that might be significant. Often, significance is spurious, however, and Lykken (1968) has stated that statistical significance is the least important attribute of good research. A third problem that Kamhi mentioned is the problem that, as N increases, so will sources of variability that cannot be identified, recognized, or categorized. Thus, it is more likely that one will in fact find no significant trends, and consequently commit a Type II (beta) error by failing to reject the null hypothesis.

Longitudinal research, which will be discussed in the next chapter, introduces its own biases towards small N. Since such studies require subjects who are willing to tolerate major intrusions into their lives, sometimes for a considerable period of time, and who may also be required to participate in substantial ways in the data collection process, sampling biases of various sorts may be introduced. For example, subjects who volunteer their children for such studies may differ from those who do not in motivation and personality (Achenbach 1978: 184), and their children may likewise be more verbal and outgoing. Since attrition is much more of a possibility in longitudinal studies, the size of N may change over the course of the research period. One can of course compensate by obtaining a larger sample than needed (Wells 1985 did so), but if attrition does occur and subjects need to be added or eliminated from the pool, a further bias is introduced: on what basis does one add or eliminate?

Other biases which affect not just number but other subject variables might be mentioned here. Some of these biases may be unknown, as when teachers or even the researchers themselves make the selection of subjects and introduce their prejudices. Screening and pre-testing of subjects may introduce an undesirable degree of homogeneity. There is some debate about whether heterogeneity (as in Wells's study) or homogeneity (as experimental approaches often assume) is in fact more desirable. Finally, selection may favor older subjects simply because the problems of interpretation and transcription with very young subjects are so great. Mere logistics, in longitudinal data collection, thus often favors small numbers of possibly self-selected subjects whose representativeness may be a problem.

Finally, large N studies may be criticized for obscuring individual differences when these may be important foci. Nelson's identification of referential and expressive styles of language development (1973) and Peters's (1977) of gestalt and analytic strategies are examples. Wherever description takes precedence over explanation, and often where naturalistic approaches take precedence over experimental, small N has tended to be in favor. Such studies are usually not designed in such a way that they are amenable to statistical analysis, not just because the N is too small, but because deduction is not the goal. Very often, in fact, the notion of 'design' is somewhat poorly applied to these studies. Rather, small N studies in CLR tend to be exploratory analyses which serve the essential functions of (1) providing descriptive groundwork, and (2) suggesting possible correlations to be systematically examined in subsequent research, usually with a larger sample population and with greater attempts at control of other sources of variability.

While the role of small N studies as pilot projects is an essential one, researchers often make the mistake of then over-generalizing their results and making what Schaerlaekens called 'audacious' claims about language universals (Schaerlaekens 1973: 19). Used with caution, however, small N studies have pursued quite useful intentions in CLR. Moskowitz (1970), for example, demonstrated that, based on a study of three children, there is no single strategy (of features, oppositions, or rules) that children adopt in the acquisition of phonological structure. Volterra and Taeschner (1978) studied three children and suggested a progression of three stages by which the child becomes bilingual, stages which may then become hypotheses to explore in a larger sample. Figueira (1984) presented a case study of the use of causativity by one child learning Portuguese, a study whose usefulness is apparent when compared to other studies of children's acquisition of causativity in other languages.

Small N studies thus have served four purposes in CLR. First, as noted, they are pilot studies which enable a researcher to refine the description and analysis of data for use on a larger sample. Second, they are valuable sources of information about idiosyncratic language development, as in the case of 'Genie' (Curtiss 1977, for example). Here one hopes never to have a larger sample, and yet a myriad of hypotheses about normal linguistic development may be suggested by such case studies. In this form, CLR is closest methodologically to medicine, from which it arose via psychology. Similarly, single-subject studies in communicative disorders often serve to document intervention strategies for a given subject whose pathologies may be in a unique array (Wickstrom et al. 1985: 285).

A small N study may be used as an attempt to extend another small N study, as a form of replication, or as a way of determining the applicability of conclusions or methods in other contexts, or with other languages. For example, the difficulties inherent in measuring mean length of utterance (see chapter 6) will appear with even a single subject. Of related significance, finally, is the use of small N to dispute claims of universality, although this may depend upon the strength of the claim, and, for example, whether universality simply means that a strategy is 'universally available', a weak claim (Ferguson 1983).

Defense of large sample sizes

We have already noted the importance of large samples for statistical analysis. In fact, some of the criticisms aimed at large N studies have less to do with size than with limitations imposed by inferential thinking itself: the tendency to turn away from fact-finding into cause-locating; the requirement that what is being examined be measurable (and the consequent requirement for precise categories of analysis, generally pre-determined, which may therefore not reflect the child's language so much as the adult's system into which data are perhaps forced to fit); and the bias toward structural (rather than the fuzzier functional) approaches with cross-sectional and/or experimental designs. It is true that large N studies may be expensive – Wells (1985) described well the staggering record-keeping demands of a longitudinal study with a large sample. However, many of the objections to large N can be dismissed, and some of the problems can be solved.

For researchers concerned with individuality, Siegel and Young (1987) emphasized that individual scores are still available, as is information about the number of subjects whose performance was at variance or in accordance with the norm. Statistical treatment often can suggest phenomena requiring further investigation when very high levels of significance are juxtaposed with very small behavioral changes. Siegel and Young stressed that one must realize that neither large nor small N studies are expected to yield the conclusion that any one treatment is effective for all subjects. As for clinical applicability, much basic research yields a great deal of clinically relevant material, although it may not have been designed with this goal in mind. It is not clear that so-called 'applied research' is in fact more significant in the long run for practical applications than basic research which develops new assessment tools or performance measures (consider MLU, for example).

Some of the problems of unwieldiness of large N can be overcome with compromise. Accumulation of longitudinal data with a smaller N is viewed as an acceptable alternative to using larger N and gathering fewer utterances for a shorter period of time, although utterances from the same child are less likely to be independent than utterances from a large group (Woods, Fletcher and Huges 1986: 106). Relaxation of standards for homogeneity is another solution, especially since homogeneity may actually diminish generality of the conclusions. Furthermore, it is not necessary that exactly the same types of data be gathered for every subject over exactly the same time period (Siegel and Young 1987: 197–8). Large N is in effect required by experimental approaches precisely because data are not naturalistic; the relationship between design and sample size is in this case both practical and necessary. Sheer numbers are required to compensate for the possible artificiality of the data. Longitudinal studies favor small N less for necessary than for practical reasons, yet as recording techniques and analytical procedures become increasingly mechanized sample size may also increase as logistical problems diminish (see also chapter 5).

Gender of subjects

Wickstrom et al. (1985) reported that, in 93 per cent of the articles in forty journals of communicative disorders, special education, and psychology which they reviewed, sex (i.e., gender) of subjects was reported. Age was the only variable reported more often. Clearly, gender is seen to be an important subject characteristic which may influence analysis and interpretation of results. Indeed, the issue of gender has developed into something of a controversy in CLR, especially concerning the presumed superiority of females in rate and other features of language development. Lynch (1983), in a review of the literature on gender differences, uncovered many studies which report that differences which may appear in language use or development seldom reach statistical significance, despite the fact that there are significant differences between boys and girls in socialization and the form and content of language directed at them (Lewis 1972; Lewis and Cherry 1977; Ling and Ling 1974; Mccaulay 1978; Winitz 1959). More recently, Kenney and Prather (1986) found that pre-school boys of a certain age did make significantly more articulation errors than girls, but otherwise were not inferior. Since most of the research has demonstrated that differences between the genders are not significant, one would think that it matters little whether this variable is reported and, furthermore, that it should be an unimportant variable in subject selection.

The problem is that apparent differences persist. Edwards remarked that one must be careful in interpreting studies of children whose sex is known, especially where the behavior (e.g., language) is subject to sex stereotyping. Similarly, people sometimes assign sex to unknown children, often erroneously, on the basis of similar stereotypes (Edwards 1979: 126). It is commonplace to hear linguists, educators, speech pathologists, and parents make reference to the superior linguistic ability of the typical girl. It is here that applied outcomes of research are dramatically exhibited. To take just one example, I once brought my then fifteen-month-old son to a speech and hearing clinic for evaluation, out of a concern that his history of chronic otitis media was to blame for his poor localization of sound and his articulation difficulties. More than one professional assured me that he was doing well to speak as much as he did, given not only that he was a second child, but a boy!

Until the discrepancy between folk wisdom and research findings is completely eliminated, one would be wise to report gender of subjects in research, even where N is small and no statistical analyses are planned, but especially where N is large enough that gender might be investigated (as part of a study with another focus) as an independent variable. Ideally, research should be designed with equal numbers of males and females. In CLR, this is quite often not the case, and in contrast to Wickstrom et al. I found that in over 35 per cent of articles reviewed, gender is not even reported. Where it is reported, studies tend to favor females as subjects. This is curious, given that a somewhat higher precentage of males actually exists in the population of children under six. Ultimately, the issue of gender differences needs to be addressed in studies using an enormous number of both male and female subjects.

Sibling position

Subjects are seldom selected or examined on the basis of sibling position (but cf. Wells 1985), nor is this often reported, and yet birth order seems a more likely significant characteristic than gender. The greater amount of time that a first-born spends in interaction with parents, as opposed to siblings, may enhance development, although spacing between siblings is an important mitigating factor. The myth, if indeed it is a myth, that subsequent-born children are slower in language development and generally less verbal is at least as pervasive as perceived female superiority. In this case, however, there is some research to support the belief.

Clearly, children are exposed to many different linguistic environments, one of which is that provided by home and family. Some studies, reported in Powers (1971), affirm that sibling position affects speech and language development. Twins between the ages of five and ten, for example, do not articulate as well as either singletons or only-children of the same ages (Davis 1937), suggesting that the presence of a sibling of like age exposes the child to a greater amount of misarticulated language. Beckey (1942) found that children with delayed 'speech' (i.e., language) tended to be youngest, suggesting that an older sibling introduces factors into the environment to which a first-born or only child is not exposed. Many parents, indeed, will comment that their youngest children talked late, and will often attribute this to the fact that the child had his or her needs met so efficiently by the older sibling that verbal communication was superfluous, at least for the first eighteen to twenty-four months.

On the other hand, evidence to the contrary also exists. Irwin (1952) found no significant differences in speech sound development between only children and those with older siblings. Since therefore, evidence is somewhat contradictory, and birth order may or may not be a significant variable, subject selection must cautiously proceed on the assumption that it ought to be controlled. In fact, this variable has been less studied than gender, and were such information supplied in research reports, post-priori kinds of analyses could be performed using sibling position as an IV. Samples which differ significantly with respect to birth order of subject may be one reason why attempts at replication sometimes fail, or why expected results in an original study are not always obtained.

Age of subjects

Where it is assumed to be related to change, age has sometimes been criticized as a subject variable (Wohlwill 1973: 24). Structuralist positions such as those of Piaget or Werner assume that age is only one dimension among many in which behavior may change. Radical behaviorists object on the grounds that age itself does not cause change, but that change is the result of other elements which happen to require the passage of time. More general objections are that some aspects of behavior may be related to age but demand a different analysis – age-change relationships, since causally bereft, are non-explanatory, and the significant degree of individual variation which occurs makes consistency of age-related functions virtually impossible to obtain (Wohlwill 1973: 24–5; he also cited Kessen 1960).

Despite these objections, change with respect to age is considered fundamental in developmental research. It is the most often reported subject variable, appearing in all of the reports reviewed by Wickstrom et al. (1985), and in 99 per cent of the CLR reports surveyed which are discussed in chapter 7. It is clear that development is quite firmly associated with age in the minds of practitioners, even if the two are not directly or causally related.

One must therefore ask how decisions concerning age of subjects are made. Typically, an investigator wants to describe or explain the (range of) structures or functions of some features of a child's language. For some, the focus may actually be on the development of these, implying a change over time in the structure or function or even in the categories of analysis themselves, either quantitatively or qualitatively. If one's focus is developmental in this sense, it is necessary to select subjects of a sufficient range in age that such changes may be clearly exhibited in the face of individual variation in rate of development; otherwise, one must follow the subjects for a longer period of time. On the other hand, a great many studies are undertaken which actually make no developmental claims, but are essentially descriptive of a given point in language acquisition. One might say these represent the 'child language' rather than the 'language development' perspective. Nevertheless, these points are usually associated with ages, and a convincing case can be made that even descriptive studies presuppose a developmental view. However, in a descriptive study the selection of subjects by age is much less critical, since the goal is only to characterize a point in time. The criterion for selection is often some other variable such as mean length of utterance or years of formal schooling (see chapters 6 and 7).

Cross-sectional, age-based studies ought in fact to be neutral with respect to development. This is because, although one may be making measurements of differences between one age group and the next, one is not in a position to make claims about the transition from one level or group to the next; yet this is perhaps the most intriguing aspect of the study of children. For this reason, Achenbach (1978: 185) has cautioned against generalizing from cross-sectional results to longitudinal or developmental conclusions, since sampling biases may be present which would lead one to attribute differences between groups to change due to age, when the differences may in fact originate in some other variable. Also, since the populations defined by a variable such as age cannot by any means be considered unchanging, the set of scores obtained from the subjects may present difficulties for the static nature of certain statistical models such as analysis of variance. When age is used as an IV, as in typical developmental research, some claim that it is in effect more appropriate to utilize essentially descriptive, rather than inferential, statistics (Wohlwill 1973: 20–1).

A few additional issues concerning the age variable deserve at least brief attention, especially where 'stage' descriptive studies are undertaken. Such studies typically involve limited numbers of subjects, and so it is doubtful that any single investigation can paint an accurate picture of the stage–age relationship. Such studies consequently pose two problems. First, how can they be transformed into developmental evidence if one cannot be certain of the degree to which the subjects represent a given stage? Chances are that variability within groups will be as great as that between groups. Despite this, the temptation is often hard to resist for changing one's essentially descriptive conclusions into developmental claims.

Second, because of the relationship between small N and single-age investigations, it is often the case that such studies make divergent or opposing claims from the current theory under construction. One need only examine such single-subject, single-age studies as Peters (1977) or Scollon (1979) to see how these – for better or worse – conflict with existing explanations. Yet little can be said about theory-data conflicts until the results are replicated with large numbers of subjects of comparable developmental levels.

There may also be a built-in tendency for single-subject, single-age studies to give the impression of subject precocity, for two reasons. First, having only one or two subjects allows the researcher freedom to record much more data, including the most advanced developments in the child's language (Braunwald and Breslin 1979: 40, 27). Second, single-subject, single-age studies are often based on the researcher's own offspring who, being the children of academicians, may indeed be more verbally advanced than the norm. As Fletcher discussed, two sampling requirements in fact exist. One is that a representative sample of children be obtained, the other that the utterances of any one child be representative of that child (1985: 11). Decisions about number and age of subjects may reflect which requirement the researcher is most concerned with.

When it comes to genuine developmental studies, researchers have a more challenging situation in choosing subjects of the appropriate age since so much variability within an age group exists. Brown (1973) stated that it was because of their awareness of such variability that his research team did not select subjects matched for chronological age. Eve was eighteen months, Adam and Sarah were twenty-seven months, and yet the mean lengths of their utterances and the lengths of their longest utterances were equivalent. He reported also that Eve's speech developed so much more rapidly than Adam and Sarah's that ten months of her transcripts could be compared with twenty months of theirs (Brown 1973: 53). Note that the abandonment of age as a critical variable simply means that, instead, one must come up with a different basis for comparison (see chapter 6). While MLU has been used quite frequently, it is by far a much more complex variable to identify.

Many practising scholars agree that of particular interest to CLR should be the period during which first words emerge, usually the last quarter of the first year. Nevertheless, most investigations have focused on the three- to five-year-old child in whom language has been fairly well established. Our notions of development in language have in this way been prejudiced by the assumed equation of 'language' with 'syntax', which has in turn restricted studies of younger children, although this has been less true in the most recent research. Similarly, the pretheoretical expectation that major developments in language occur prior to the age of five or six has made it less common to investigate development in older children.

Two future tasks for CLR practitioners concerning age of subjects are to utilize larger numbers of subjects in single-age studies, and to develop research which includes a wider age range, and pushes outward to the boundaries of linguistic and general communicative development (i.e. to children under two, and over six, years of age). The field needs to make up its mind whether or not it is a developmental one. Other issues that concern age and various subject variables are relevant to the question of measurement of subjects, and will be taken up in that section.

Other demographic and developmental variables

Other variables presumed to be potentially influential in development are often specified. Socioeconomic status, reported in only 5 per cent of the studies surveyed by Wickstrom et al. (1985), nevertheless is considered significant by many researchers. Wells (1985) found that formative influences of the father, such as education and occupational status, which are related to socioeconomic status, are somewhat powerful in predicting a child's rate of language development, although this is largely true only for extremes of family background (Wells 1985: 346, 349). For Bernstein, important differences existed in the form of language when middle- and working-class children were compared. Some of course, have challenged this view, maintaining that, among other things, the term 'restricted code' was value-laden rather than descriptive. Furthermore, in the case of working-class Black children in the United States, many of the impressions of 'disadvantaged' backgrounds and 'restricted' communicative abilities were artefacts of the interview situation itself, in which a white, adult researcher plied the naturally suspicious young subject with questions. It was no wonder the youth appeared to be reticent. In applied areas such as communicative disorders, socioeconomic status has been an issue whenever it is associated with non-standard dialects. This may influence measures of linguistic ability. For example, the Developmental Sentence Scoring procedure developed by Lee (1974) is still rather commonly used (at least in the States) to assess morphological and syntactic development in pre-school children, and yet utterances which are wholly grammatical in certain non-standard dialects, such as those which omit the copula or auxiliary *be*, cannot be given 'sentence points' (Lively 1984). The resulting scores would favor children from socioeconomic backgrounds in which standard English is spoken.

Some variables in the selection of subjects pertain to their abilities, where these are not the DV. In particular, dissatisfaction with the use of age as a base-line may prompt investigators to explore alternative classifications such as mental age or linguistic development of some sort. Some of these are suspect, as in the case of mental age, which is not only 'intrinsically correlated' with chornological age in children, but is also a 'highly heterogeneous' and therefore dubious metric for use as an IV (Wohlwill 1973: 27–9). Since MLU may also hint of circularity, it may be wise, unless one is deliberately trying to determine what other measurements correlate with it, to avoid it altogether, at least as an IV (see also chapter 6, which contains a lengthier discussion of the problems involved in calculation of MLU). This is not to say that such measures of ability, if available, do not have their place in the selection of subjects and the reporting of data. Rather, it is their status as IVs which one must scrutinize. The same can be said of the more 'pragmatically' based measures.

Any of a variety of other variables which might be associated with communicative development are potentially confounding or influential. (Wells even looked at factors such as birth month.) If cultural differences exist among subjects, even those from the same linguistic and socioeconomic environments, these must be noted. They are not always easy to detect. In some sense, a family in itself represents a sort of subculture, with its own belief systems and attitudes towards both language and silence. These attitudes and beliefs may be manifested at the simplest level, as in the manner in which the parent typically addresses the child or even the amount of speech which appears in the corpus. Is the language directed at the child, for example, structured in such a way that his or her responses are limited? While children clearly are recipients of a variety of types of communication, one style may be dominant, especially in particular ethnic groups or with one or another caregiver. Such potentially important features need at least to be noted, and ultimately studied, preferably without qualitative judgments. Ethnomethodological frameworks presuppose that such sub-cultural variables can be identified and described, and their relationship to communicative development explored. The role of educational institutions, with regard to older subjects, or of caregivers other than parents with whom children spend a large proportion of their time, must not be minimized in this regard.

Finally, one should never fail to screen for medical or other abnormalities, such as psychiatric disorders, chronic otitis media, or features of medical history such as Reye Syndrome, hydrocephalus, or premature birth. All of these may potentially influence the data one seeks to collect. Wickstrom et al. (1985) reported that 83 per cent of the articles they surveyed reported a diagnosis; in work on normal child language development, one might expect at least a word of assurance that all subjects are, apparently, normal.

Where description has not even been adequately achieved, much less explanation, it is essential that subjects be selected with rigorous standards. In the non-ideal world in which CLR must be pursued, age is still the best IV for effective developmental-functional approaches, for it is at the very least a base-line against which changes can be consistently revealed despite 'noise' from other sources of variance (Wohlwill 1973: 33). If the changes we observe are real, then they will persist, and thorough descriptions of many conceivably significant variables will enhance our attempts to make and test hypotheses about just which characteristics are relevant for language acquisition.

A field such as CLR, with its diverse disciplinary affiliations and the non-cohesive nature of its theory and methods, stands to gain much in the credibility and adequacy of its descriptions, and ultimately explanations, whenever practitioners can agree on any approach. Selection and description of subjects, without whom there would be no data, seem apt places to start.

5 Data Collection

Disciplinary influences on data

The nature of the research process, particularly the collection and analysis of data, may be swayed as much by the social conditions of disciplinary affiliations as anything more noble. The number of practitioners from different fields which CLR boasts is certainly a major reason for its peculiar blend of methodologies and the disheartening diversity of practices. Behind the disciplinary ranks are, however, conditions that affect all inquiry, and which Whitely (1985) has called differences of 'strategic' verses 'functional' dependence and 'strategic' versus 'technical' task uncertainty. Technical certainty concerns replicability of procedures and the degree to which interpretation of results is unambiguous. It is high in natural sciences, but low where lay influences are strong, as in the social sciences, and certainly in CLR. Where there are many funding agencies, strategic task uncertainty may occur. It concerns ill-defined priorities regarding which problems to solve and how to assess the significance of results. This type of uncertainty, too, plagues CLR. Concerning dependence, the borrowing of ideas and procedures in narrow but related areas, as between certain sub-fields of psychology and linguistics, makes for high functional dependence. Strategic dependence, on the other hand, refers to the extent that one researcher must persuade others of the value of his or her work. This type of dependence is high in theoretically coherent fields (physics, economics), but low in fields such as chemistry and sociology (Simpson 1985: 658), and certainly CLR. Surely strategic dependence has increased over the years in the field, given the proliferation of justifications, criticisms, and defensive responses from authors concerning their work. It may be that editorial standards, rather than theoretical coherence, have played a strong role in forcing strategic dependence.

In general, the unification of the field with respect to acceptable data and their collection is the least likely to occur where CLR, and psycholinguistics in general, has tried to be faithful to the methods of modern (American) linguistics. Some of the difficulties in this regard have been mentioned already, and they can be summarized in the view expressed by Goldman-Eisler that a description of a language is not likely to be a good candidate as a scientific hypothesis about the psychological processes of the language user. Not only does such a notion confuse grammatical rules and mental processes, but it has depended upon contrived data, where the data of psycholinguistics must of necessity be dynamic and situational (Goldman-Eisler 1972: 69). Although Chomsky and his followers were probably not guided by any such confusion, data in CLR have nevertheless contrasted with much general linguistic data by including large amounts of spontaneous utterances collected in naturalistic or semi-naturalistic settings (Ochs 1979: 9). Nor, of course, is it enough merely to require such data which, usually too raw to be helpful, must then be transcribed, coded, measured, analyzed, and interpreted. At every stage troubles lurk and ultimately one's interpretive-theoretical tasks may be only as fragile or firm as the recording equipment employed, instruments of measurement, categories of coding and modes of analysis, or even the degree of confidence one has in the data. Given all the disciplinary and extra-disciplinary factors which affect research processes, it is surprising that any field manages to achieve some kind of unity. Often that unity begins in the area of data collection rather than theory.

Methods of recording

In CLR, where it is not always so much the language itself we seek to understand as its origins in the minds of children, we are limited from the outset because the very thing we wish to view is not directly accessible, i.e., not a 'first-order' entity. Given that we have no direct data, the second obstacle to research is that speech fades much more rapidly than we are able to perform even the most rudimentary analyses. The evolution of devices to accomplish the end of 'freezing' dynamic data into a static, somewhat lifeless record is an evolution only of a sort, for the oldest forms, rather than being cast off as newer techniques are invented, have continued to be utilized. Diaries are still popular tools, and are sometimes used in tandem with more sophisticated electronic devices. In many ways, one's method of recording is selected according to factors of different levels of theoretical value. The purposes of the analysis, but also such matters as the amount of funding available, help to determine the choice of recording equipment.

Diary studies

Assumptions and advantages

The most enduring form of record-keeping in CLR has been the diary study. As does any method, this means has underlying assumptions as well as advantages and disadvantages. Although it has been less popular in recent years than audiotaping, it has survived in the more limited forms of supplementary note-taking of various sorts (Braunwald and Breslin 1979; Fletcher 1985).

The primary assumption of any recording technique is that the behaviors and actions that appear outwardly are our only major access to the inner life of the child (Stern 1930: 33). From the beginning, the diary study was a commitment to longitudinal analysis (Braunwald and Breslin 1979: 24), and for this reason it has been rather out of favor in the USA and other areas where the impact of experimental social sciences is greatest. Whereas experimental approaches demand relatively low probabilities for verification, and changes of a relatively large magnitude, the diary study documents changes of a minute order which can only be gleaned by means of continual, day-to-day monitoring (Braunwald and Breslin 1979: 41). Thus it is clear that one's notions about the nature of development are interdependent with the recording technique. One-time contacts with subjects, such as may occur in experimental or cross-sectional analyses, may make development appear to occur in spurts where a longitudinal record, especially daily dairy entries, displays the gradual ebb and flow of development.

A third assumption, albeit one which appears to be changing, is that diary studies are primarily studies of language production. Stern strongly emphasized that records of spontaneous behavior provide much clearer insights into the child's actual knowledge than do responsive and experimentally elicited behaviors (1930: 38–9). Bloom (1974b, 288–9) noted also the production bias, particularly in the early diary studies such as Guillaume (1927) and Leopold (1939) – a bias resulting from apparent 'skepticism' concerning children's comprehension and a failure to record very much after the first observation of those responses which seemed to indicate emerging comprehension.

Diary studies still represent an alternative to the experimental studies which, for the study of individual development, Stern felt to be so inferior (1930: 39). More recently, however, the dairy has been used as a supplement to other forms which include experimental approaches. Greenfield and Smith remarked that diaries can be complementary to more formal sessions which involve a limited time, allowing the researcher to view more accurately the child's development (1976: 32–3). Experimental data can complement diary studies in two ways. Experimentally tested hypotheses may be based on data originally recorded in the diary; conversely, the diary may serve as a source of verification for experimentally derived data. Other media sources, included interval-sampling techniques, also combine well with diary records to form a fruitful and varied source of data (Braunwald and Breslin 1979: 27). The extent to which data in published diaries have continued to be used by other researchers testifies to their significance in the history of CLR (Fletcher 1985: 8–9), whether combined with other data sources or not.

Definition of the diary study

The diary record, defined as a regularly kept journal or protocol in written form, has been distinguished from the diary study, a much larger project for which the written diary record serves as nucleus (Braunwald and Breslin 1979: 24). The diary might therefore include various forms of note-taking, as long as these conform to a format and are kept on a regular basis. The distinction between a diary record and primary or supplementary note-taking is that, first of all, diary entries tend to be made at more frequent intervals; second, the main observer in the case of diary records, the keeper of the diary, is generally the primary caregiver who has a well-established, intimate relationship with the child being observed; third, the diary is usually more comprehensive than note-taking; and fourth, the diary is a longitudinal commitment usually to a single subject (Fletcher 1985: 9).

Although the observational task is in some ways more accurately and objectively accomplished by someone with training in the field, the ideal observer is actually the caregiver (usually mother, followed by other relatives) precisely because of the intimate knowledge she has of the child (Stern 1930: 35). The most well-known records in diary form were in fact kept by persons who had both characteristics of professional and parent: the Sterns, Leopold, Velten, and N.V. Smith, to name a few (Fletcher 1985: 8, also lists extant diary studies). Although apparently ideal, such a situation does introduce some difficulties, especially in answer to the question of purpose. While the lay person may keep a diary 'for personal reasons' or 'to help a scientific study', the linguist or psychologist may answer too narrowly. This may affect the form of the study and eliminate its primary advantages. In the case of records kept for so-called 'scientific' purposes, the wealth of the material, while exhilarating, is less important than its reliability and objectivity (Stern 1930: 37). The lay person may on occasion fail to distinguish observation from interpretation, but this may actually be a greater problem for someone whose perspective is guided by theoretical and pre-theoretical assumptions and expectations. Furthermore, since diary studies do have the potential for recording the child's most advanced developments, which could give the impression of precocity, these behaviors may actually be quite ordinary (Braunwald and Breslin 1979: 27, 40). On the other hand, as noted previously, the child of a CLR pratitioner may indeed be linguistically precocious, especially if first-born; so one must be cautious in theorizing based on such data and in using the record in any way for the establishment of norms.

The ideal diarist is familiar enough with linguistic systems to be able to recognize new developments in the child's speech, but also familiar enough with the child's background to determine whether a given utterance is the result of extension of a rule or of exposure. Parents' observations are valuable in the latter regard (Berko and Brown 1960: 542, 520). Leopold has for these reasons produced a diary which remains a standard against which others might be compared. He was successful not only in describing development in each of the major linguistic sub-systems, but even then of comparing it in his two daughters (Berko and Brown 1960: 529). By the same token, any human observer has the difficulty of recording not necessarily a set of behaviors so much as a culture-specific interpretation of them (Summerfield 1983: 4–5); that is to say, he or she may make an emic rather than an etic record. This is abundantly clear to anyone who has tried to teach naive students phonetic transcription and observed how their own dialect often serves as a filter for their perceptions of sound. The cross-cultural value of diary studies may thus be compromised, and generally speaking, the investigator must determine in which direction to err. Many researchers are led to abandon imperfect human observers wherever possible and turn to more neutral inorganic mechanisms; yet, as Fassnacht remarked, 'certain data can only be represented through the human perceptual system' (1982: 4). Such representation, in the case of language data, must either occur at the level of recording, or at the level of transcription and coding. Again, the individual researcher must determine where to wrestle with the problem.

Format

The necessity of having thorough, objective, reliable, and self-justifying records introduces several requirements of form which have been discussed in various (though often far-flung) places in the literature. One of the most essential but troublesome features is a clear separation between the outward, observed behaviors and any conclusions drawn from these. The latter must always be justified both by child nature in general and actual observation of the particular child (Stern 1930: 35). It is preferable to have actually distinct parts of the diary record for each type of information. Although there is risk, in this regard, that the so-called naive observer may provide too 'rich' an interpretation (Brown 1973), there is also risk that the trained but impartial (to the child) observer might under-characterize the child's abilities. Some solution to this dilemma is to use two or more observers (Oksaar 1983: 54), who either gather data simultaneously or at regular intervals to supplement the diary record of the parent.

A second essential feature of written records is supplementary information concerning the child's general health, heredity, and environment (see chapter 4). Stern felt this should include the child's race; social class; siblings, friends, relatives, and others who influence the child, especially their dialects; the parents' ages; and a description of the location and nature of the child's living quarters (1930: 39–40). One should also keep track in this section of the record of routines in the child's life, unusual events which might have occurred, and the identification of referents, especially those for which the child uses idiosyncratic names. For example, in my own records I have noted that my son referred to a diaper as [bapi], and my daughter called any piece of fruit 'ball'.

Organizationally, the record must be kept chronologically, although cross-indexing of various sorts is extremely helpful. If more than one child is involved, Stern recommended keeping a separate record-book for each child, but this makes it problematic when the children interact with one another. Must the interaction be entered in both records? Another solution is the provision of separate columns on a given page for each participant (also a solution for transcription; see below, and Ochs 1979: 50–9). During solitary play by one child, only a single column will be used. At other times several columns may be required, which has implications for the size and orientation of the paper.

Modern technology now makes it possible for several records to be entered onto the computer and cross-filed. Certain text-editing programs may then allow the researcher to retrieve all instances of a given structure or word; or to align two or more records side-by-side or top-and-bottom, so that, for example, one can compare the child's speech with different participants. In general, the computer has opened up a number of intriguing possibilities for storing as well as organizing and analyzing data (discussed in the next chapter).

Stern urged observers to record the age of the child month by month. Recently, practitioners have tended to record age more specifically, even to the day, using the format years: months; days, e.g., 1:8;19 (Braunwald and Breslin 1979: 31), or in weeks for very young children. However, I must confess to being somewhat confounded by reports of a child's age such as '68 weeks' or '53 months', and I always convert these in my own mind to 1:4 (roughly) or 4:5. The age is placed at the top of each page representing a separate observation day.

At minimum, the communicative record itself must include, for each entry, the act of communication and some indication of whether it was spontaneous, imitative, or responsive; the situational context – e.g. 'K. is at the kitchen table trying to put puzzle shapes into a small mailbox while mother helps'; and accompanying behaviors, gestures, or reactions (Braunwald) and Breslin 1979: 30–1). Greenfield and Smith also advocated the recording of expansions or interpretations along with all the situational cues on which these are based (as noted, interpretations should be kept in a separate place); and, in addition, all the relevant adjacent communication (1976: 33), since this also provides clues to meaning which the analysis may subsequently require.

In general, utterances are transcribed broadly, except where unintelligibility, non-canonical words, or 'sound-play' are the case (Greenfield and Smith 1976: 33; Ochs 1979: 45), even though an utterance may be recognized as sound-play only after it is too late to capture it phonetically. This indicates the value of supplemental recording on audiotape, especially if there is a chance that a phonological study will be undertaken. I am personally skeptical of the value of diary records alone for phonological analyses; Smith (1973) was successful, but for many people it is extremely difficult to make rapid, on-site phonetic transcriptions. Stern suggested developing a shorthand for the child's longer utterances (1930: 41). It is always a problem to keep up with an especially verbal child, and thus the diary record may be better suited to younger, holophrastic, or at least relatively reticent subjects. Any abbreviatory devices must be explicated somewhere in the record if it is to be of value for other researchers; certainly in this day one needs to approach data collection more altruistically with the assumption that data may be shared and benefit the entire field. Finally, any discontinuities in the record must be noted, or temporary changes in the observer, since these may affect the conclusions one draws from the data (Stern 1930: 30–40).

As Braunwald and Breslin have expressed, the format of the diary record can never achieve the ideal, but will always be a compromise between theory and practice (1979: 28). This is clearly true of all research, hence the assumption that, in the abstract, different formats of the same method or even different collection devices altogether are of potentially the same value. The essential factor in data collection is not whether a method appears to be 'subjective' or 'objective', but rather the consistency of its relationship to what it represents (Fassnach 1982: 8).

Some more detailed aspects of format considerations are also discussed in the next chapter, in the section on transcription. Meanwhile, having already noted some problems relative to the observer in diary studies, we must articulate some of the other potential disadvantages of written recording methods.

Disadvantages of notes and diaries

Notes and diaries, especially when providing the sole record, can be potentially troublesome forms of capturing data. The foremost problem is selectivity. Although all methods of recording are selective to some degree, the difficulty with human observation is in assessing what types of knowledge brought to the process are explicit and what types implicit. Humans clearly have information about an object of investigation prior to any observation (Fassnacht 1982: 11), and it is virtually impossible to make this information fully explicit. It is not desirable, of course, to eliminate it.

A second problem is that of planning, which must be thorough, particularly with respect to plans for redundancy of data. This is especially crucial if a non-diarist will be reviewing the record in order to determine intentionality of communication; or for strict and consistent use of a notational system, so that changes indicate development rather than shoddy record-keeping or a change in observer; for providing sufficient supplementary information for interpreting utterances weeks, months, or years after their having been recorded; and for connecting language with other development should this be desired (Braunwald and Breslin 1979: 29, 33).

Third, it is often difficult to determine, when few examples of a form occur, whether the form is an idiosyncracy, a dialectal variant, or more common. Chances are, unless built-in control of the situations of recording has been attempted, speech occurred in such a wide variety of contexts that there would be little hope of duplicating just the right conditions in order to make comparisons with other subjects (Berko and Brown 1960: 544). Velten (1943), for example, was unable to obtain from his daughter data concerning all possible phonemic contrasts. An experimentalist might have intervened, inventing toys for her to fetch such as a [po] and a [bo] (Berko and Brown 1960: 529–30). Related to this problem is the concern that diary studies in general are less exact and more subjective than, say, the experimental method (Braunwald and Breslin 1979: 28), subject to the respective limitations of the non-professional or professional diarist. However, some have felt that it is pointless to compare the merits of observation and experimentation in this way, since they have so little in common. Observation is data collection, experimentation is essentially data production. One cannot progress, if this is the proper word, to experimentation in a given field except after a very long period of fact-finding, primarily through observation. Some in fact believe that psychology embarked prematurely into experimentation. Furthermore, different methods such as observation and experimentation are potentially neutral, but have come to represent, and thus become 'whipping boys' for, different theoretical positions (Fassnacht 1982: 35–7).

Fourth, Fletcher believed that diary studies are not as well suited to syntactic as to phonological analysis. This is because of the problem of increased selectivity in recording as the child's output increases (1985: 9). On the other hand, phonetic transcription, required for any kind of thorough phonological analysis, can be equally time-consuming, especially in the first year when the child produces a number of sounds not necessarily in the repertoire of the target language and for which no symbols exist. This is further complicated by the problems of capturing prosodic features of utterances, should one wish to treat these (see Crystal 1978 on problems in the analysis of intonation).

Finally, diary studies are a major invasion of privacy which may be disruptive to the parent–child relationship (Braunwald and Breslin 1979: 41). Some children (my daughter, for example) may simply not tolerate mother's being busy with note-taking. They are considerably time-consuming since data are often gathered daily and they may be expensive, particularly if the diarist is paid for his or her efforts, although, interestingly, CLR has progressed over the past fifteen to twenty years without, as a rule, paying its subjects. Finally, more than any other form, note and diary records tend to be exceedingly voluminous, which can create enormous organizational difficulties and contribute to a high degree of strategic task uncertainty when one must ultimately assess the value of all these data. Here, the personal computer and the continually decreasing size of storage disks will be an invaluable benefit. Nevertheless, the data are still usually recorded by hand, and thus an additional step is required to transfer the data to computer; this eliminates one of the advantages of diary studies – the bypassing of transcription. For all these reasons, diaries are still by nature limited to the description of only one or two children. This in turn precludes generalization, and makes the study subject to all the limitations of small N previously discussed.

Despite these disadvantages, many people feel that the benefits of a good diary study are tantalizing, and that they outweigh the risks. Diary or supplemental note-taking methods allow one to determine, in many cases, whether the absence of a communicative behavior means it is beyond the subject's competence, simply not elicited by the situation, or absent due to motivational or attitudinal factors (Braunwald and Breslin 1979: 27). If the data can be coded and analyzed directly from the diary pages, transcription is avoided. The use of loose-leaf pages or computer disks allows for considerable flexibility in making data organization sensitive to different goals and theoretical purposes.

Most experimental and cross-sectional studies cannot be as comprehensive as the longitudinal diary study. If one conceives of CLR as the study not just of child language but of its development as well, the diary record, perhaps more than any other form, allows one to view the essential transitions of language use from one point to the next, and the dynamic, nature of these transitions (Braunwald and Breslin 1979: 41). The diarist thus has access to the developmental relationship between different 'stages', temporal or otherwise (Greenfield and Smith 1976: 32, citing Jakobson 1969). A diary study does not necessarily require any equipment other than pencil and paper, and the diarist is freer to follow the young subjects about wherever they may go. It intrudes less upon the subjects' lives in this regard. Finally, a diary study allows one to focus on the careful, methodic documentation of development as well as the ever-unraveling story of the life of an individual child in interaction with the surrounding world. In this way, as Braunwald and Breslin have noted (1979: 42), the diary study is perhaps best able to bridge the gap so apparent in CLR between the social sciences and the humanities.

Other recording methods and their disadvantages

If diary and note methods of naturalistic recording have the flaws of being selective and heavily dependent upon immediate interpretation (Prideaux 1985: 65), audiotape and videotape are almost completely non-discriminating in the events and utterances which they will capture, subject to the built-in mechanical constraints of each. In addition, scholars who advocate videotaping do so because of the need to capture non-verbal and non-vocal behaviors which contribute extensively to one's attempts to analyze and make inferences, especially about comprehension (Lloyd and Donaldson 1976: 414), but also about production. Just as it is difficult in the early years to write down all the relevant aspects of the extra-linguistic context, so in later years it becomes difficult to capture all the relevant linguistic context. The impartial video camera will record both of these and, with proper equipment, even allow behaviors to be isolated down to a fortieth of a second (Oksaar 1983: 54). These are the main reasons that, at least in some fields, videotaping has almost entirely supplanted the use of trained human recorders (Summerfield 1983: 3).

The disadvantages of videotape are numerous, however, and this is perhaps why it has not been as extensively utilized in CLR as one might expect (see chapter 7), although its popularity is increasing. The human eye is far superior to a camera lens in its visual field (Costello 1973), and humans are of course quick to react to events and sounds beyond the field of a fixed camera. A great deal of expertise is really required if one is to place and use the camera and other equipment properly. Video equipment is more intrusive than diary keeping. Although the apparata are becoming more compact, they are still bulky, somewhat heavy, and work more easily when placed in a room in a stationary position than when hand-held. Yet the space constraints may make it difficult to place a tripod, which requires more area than one sometimes expects; and, ideally, one should be able to follow subjects about from room to room to achieve both variety of situational contexts and a continuous record. The problem of the obviousness of the recording device is great, and will be discussed in greater detail presently. If one person has to operate the camera, then he or she is not free to take notes, as an ideal methodology would require, and so an extra person is often needed. This can add to the cost of a project when videotaping is already more expensive to begin with than either diary or note-taking or audiotaping. There is also some indication that subjects react more strongly to being video taped than audiotaped (Renne, Dowrick and Wasek 1983: 28, citing Gelso 1973); yet the mere presence of any observer can influence the child.

Schaerlaekens (1973: 21–2) discussed difficulties in audiotaping, many of which are applicable to videotaping as well. The sound or visual quality may be poorer than one might like, child reticence – especially in the case of non-supplemented audiotape – means that one could end up with a substantial amount of expensive 'dead air'; the size of microphones may be too large or small. Although most newer-model videorecorders have built-in microphones, these are typically less sensitive than is needed, and tend to pick up the sound of the motor if one is using automatic zoom. Both forms of taping must generally be transcribed prior to analysis, adding an additional selectivity process to the research. Micro-analysis is possible but can be difficult directly from videotape. Although one may need to slow and even stop action frequently, the image at best will probably quiver and at worst may flip, while resolution may be less than ideal (Scheflen, Kendon and Schaeffer 1970: 230). In this regard, motion picture film is better, although it has little else to recommend it. In addition, some researchers feel that videotape can be overused, especially when the analysis is relatively simple, and that such records may lead to over-analysis. Finally, certain behaviors, such as gestures, may be more noticeable than in direct observation (Maxwell and Pringle 1983: 35), which might in turn lead to an exaggeration of their role in the communicative event.

The specific disadvantages of audiotape, for all its apparent simplicity, are many. Although non-vocal context may play a crucial role in semantic content of the child's utterances, it cannot be captured. Audiotape without supplementation may be fine for a limited study of older children; there is no justification for relying on it exclusively with children under the age of four or five – those most commonly investigated in CLR. Children of this age use non-verbal behaviors such as gestures, facial expressions, eye gaze, and body movements extensively, not only to supplement, but often to supplant speech behavior (Brannigan and Humphries 1972: 39). Fletcher reported that his subject Sophie would, based on her mother's interpretation, sometimes express negative intent without negative marking. He remarked that no other reports of this appear in the literature (1985: 77). However, this may be a gap that is to be blamed on recording methods. At least one child of my acquaintance, at the age of two, expressed negation by stating the affirmative while shaking her head back and forth. Only visual contact can capture such peculiarities, which may in fact be more common than reported. However, any study which includes phonology must have audiotaped records in addition to others, since sound quality on videorecorders is inferior to that of most audiorecorders (Summerfield 1983: 8), and it is essential to have a sound record against which to check transcriber disagreements, should these occur.

Advantages of videotaping

In contrast to the limitations of audiotaping, videorecording is an advantageous tool. The equipment is becoming increasingly compact, more automatic, and hence easier to operate. Less expertise and a shorter training period are now required for one to become familiar with the equipment. Automatic exposure meters mean that one need not have any particular knowledge of lighting, since the aperture will adjust to the ambient light, down to about ten lux or meter-candles in some cases (i.e., one foot-candle). This eliminates in turn the need for much additional lighting, unless one is recording after dusk. Some specific concerns regarding lighting will be discussed in the next section.

Many of the foremost advantages of videotaping are identical to those of diaries, with the added benefit that, if one can arrange the space in such a way as to allow the camera to record and focus automatically, it is possible for the researcher to have hands, ears, and eyes free to engage in observation and, if desired, take supplementary notes, or jot down questions to be explored later about the ongoing activity. Some equipment has two audio-channels, one of which can be used to record observers' comments (Scheflen, Kendon and Schaeffer 1970: 237). The selectivity problem is also reduced – most bias is eliminated except that which results from the camera angle or enters during analysis. Videotaping may also serve, therefore, as an important back-up system to diaries, both to balance the subjective element and to supply more detail (Braunwald and Breslin 1979: 24), since the visual record will be relatively neutral and comprehensive. The method thus has the potential for making analysis of observed phenomena highly reliable (Maxwell and Pringle 1983: 36).

There is also the advantage of instant playback. Frequently, the playback monitor is in the viewfinder itself. Using two or more cameras will allow the researcher to focus wide with one, capturing the larger context, and to zoom in with the other for focusing on an individual face. For purposes of analysis, it is then possible to superimpose one image upon another one or use a split-screen to view both images simultaneously (Wilmer 1970: 218–22). In fact, the technological potential of video equipment, especially in combination with other electronic instruments, has barely been probed in CLR.

An exception to this is the use of a microcomputer in combination with editing decks and time-code readers, developed and described by Beckwith et al. (1985). Linked with a multiplexing circuit, the combination of means allowed them to code for different behaviors with each viewing of the tape, then later merge the records. They were in turn able to observe sequential and other temporal relationships both developmentally and at micro-levels. Behaviors can be isolated within frames to one thirtieth of a second and coded with a time-code generator, as well as described via the edit mode using up to 255 characters. The data can then be stored in a file for analysis, from which they can be retrieved sequentially by means of the time code. Such a system, which uses primarily commercially available equipment, circumvents the need for extensive transcription, and also preserves the temporal relationships among behaviors (in different subjects or the same one) – something difficult to achieve through linear transcription. Clarke and Ellgring (1983) have also discussed advances in the area of computer-assisted videorecording.

Video techniques for CLR

Appraisals of state-of-the-art equipment and their operation are readily available in manuals and other publications, but certain guidelines for the selection and use of video equipment have an impact on the quality of data and of research in general.

First, for general research purposes the so-called 'camcorder' is a reasonable choice. It is relatively inexpensive and does not require a separate VCR (video cassette recorder) deck. In order to check on the quality of the image being recorded, one need merely switch modes and peer into the viewfinder. Much research time can be saved if one can adjust in advance to any problems of sound or image. Many camcorders also allow the operator to record the date, age of the child, and certain aspects of setting onto the tape for convenience in filing and organizing data.

An earphone allows the monitoring of sound quality, although experience sometimes proves that the sound is actually better during playback than it seems to be through the earphone. Most recorders have both built-in and separate, clip-on microphones; the latter, while offering somewhat better quality, can limit movement of the subject and sometimes are overly sensitive to the sound of gestures, clothing rubbing against them, and other movements. The built-in microphone is usually sufficient except for the problem of the automatic zoom motor which, of course, one need not use. One should therefore generally expect to hand-hold the equipment and supplement this with a higher-quality but less portable stationary camera. The microphone for this, or for supplementary audiotape recorders, should be suspended from the ceiling.

Although most recent models use available light, some depth of field is invariably sacrificed if ambient light is dim. This will affect quality if there is more than one person being taped and one is positioned behind the other a few feet; it may likewise be problematic if both background and foreground contain significant features of the context. A good solution is always to use well-lighted rooms or to record outdoors in daylight. The latter may pose lighting problems if the subject is in shade but the background is bright. The aperture of the lens will decrease automatically in response to the background light, and the subject will consequently be underexposed. In these circumstances one must take care to manually override the automatic exposure device. Outdoor light also tends to vary in intensity, especially on cloudy days or as daylight fades, so that the setting must be monitored periodically. Again, this is easier to do if the camera is hand-held, but this demands an observer whose only task is to operate the camera. For these reasons, outdoor taping is not usually undertaken. It is best, wherever possible, to create one's own research setting with consistency of light, textures, and space (pp. 73–4)

Portable equipment does not as a rule have interchangeable lenses, and angles on available lenses are not especially wide. In a recent session, my colleagues and I had serious difficulties keeping two two-year-olds within the angle of the lens, even though they were situated in a small room. Two cameras would have solved this problem for the most part.

Any photographer is aware of the influence of camera angle on the interpretation of a visual image. It is certainly easier to film standing up, with the lens pointed downward at the subject, but this can contribute to the sense that the child is inferior, which may in turn affect the coding of the child's language and other behavior. The best rule of thumb is to keep the camera level with the subject wherever possible (Livingstone 1953: 53). It is also best, to approach objectivity, to keep the subjects centered if there are more than one and to shoot head-on. Although this is less visually pleasing than a view composed for more depth, it allows one to record equally the behaviors of both subjects, without generating the impression that one or the other, especially in mother–child dyads, is less essential. If, for example, one were to shoot past the back of a mother's head to her child, the mother's role in the interaction might appear to be less significant than otherwise. As Summerfield put it, video-oriented researchers should beware of 'Hollywood' techniques which allow the observer's or coder's imagination to make up for any lack of comprehensiveness in the record. For this reason it is best to have camera operators who know the research area as well as, if not better than, those who are technical experts (1983: 5–6; see also Dowrick and Biggs 1983 for more comprehensive information concerning videotaped observations).

The latest available equipment allows the researcher to insert a cassette and record continuously for up to two-and-a-half hours. This raises the question of duration, and the related issue of frequency. Particularly in a longitudinal study, as much research using naturalistic data is, what is the appropriate duration of a given observation session, and how often should such sessions occur? What should the longevity of the project be? For that matter, can good naturalistic data which capture development be gathered at all without a longitudinal design?

Frequency, duration, and longevity

A survey of the literature will clearly reveal that the frequency of data collection and the longevity of a study are often arbitrarily determined. In order for one to consider what the valid variables are for data collection in, especially, a longitudinal study, one must consider again the goals of CLR in general, the aims of theory, and the ways that longitudinal or other research designs may or may not support these.

Contrary to what one might expect, longitudinal studies are by no means the norm in CLR. The majority of studies in the field are experimental or quasi-experimental, in the sense that they rely on one-time contacts with the subjects in what may or may not be a relatively controlled setting. While in recent years the proportion of naturalistic studies has been increasing, many of these are cross-sectional (see chapter 7). We have already examined the choice of experimental versus naturalistic observation methods. Given that one chooses the latter, should the design necesarily be cross-sectional or longitudinal?

It is often assumed that cross-sectional data will provide similar information to, and be comparable with, longitudinal data (S. Krashen, personal communication). However, important differences between the two approaches, some of which have already been discussed, might affect the results and their comparability. Wohwill claimed that, in psychology, over 90 per cent of developmental research has been cross-sectional. Such studies work well for major analyses in the so-called structuralist traditions which focus not so much on change as on the differences between one group and another, from which development is inferred (Wohlwill 1973: 36, 21, 20). Yet if CLR is to be concerned primarily with the question of how children become communicatively competent, it is imperative to focus on the transitions between the levels of ability. For this purpose, there are no substitutes for longitudinal data (Schwartz, Leonard, Wilcox and Folger 1980: 86).

Ideally, for a longitudinal study to serve this purpose, one would continuously trace every sort of utterance, for each subject, beginning with the first until the grammar has been internalized (Schaerlaekens 1973: 20). This view is based on the questionable assumption that major modifications of the grammatical (and other) systems serving language do not occur after a given age. Since the ideal study is therefore impossible, the recordings should certainly be made at the shortest possible intervals. If the intervals are too long, day-to-day variability may not show at all, particularly if one is observing in more or less the same situation (Oksaar 1983: 53). While an increase in frequency may allow one to decrease duration (Wells 1985: 35), one can risk decreasing frequency with a large group of children on the assumption that each subject will be at a different level, so the inherent variability and instability of systems and forms in transition will be exhibited in at least some subjects. Thus, Wells recorded every three months, but the size of his sample (128 subjects) and the longevity of the study (two-and-a-half years) were considerable, yielding over 1350 recordings of over 100 utterances each. He also noted, however, that the larger the N, the smaller amount of data one usually can afford to analyze. Similarly, the more detailed the analysis, the smaller N may need to be (Wells 1985: 9).

McNeill noted in 1970 that the typical frequency for recording seemed to be intervals of two to four weeks, although it is perhaps more common to specify that recordings were made only 'irregularly', or not to specify at all. Obviously, with the small N that usually accompanies longitudinal studies, any of these three alternatives is unacceptable for capturing variability and transitional phenomena. Concerning duration, the longer one observes, the more variety in situations, utterances, and behaviors one is likely to get (Cartwright and Cartwright 1974: 57–8), but again, duration can also be shortened with larger N. (One might say that large N can cover a multitude of sins.) In a cross-sectional study, the length of the interval between first and subsequent recording can be especially critical, since what is often decisive for a child's acquisition of a construction and its productive use is recently prior input (Moerk 1980: 116).

A third type of study combines both longitudinal and cross-sectional design and is known as a 'time-lag' strategy. It usually involves many subjects in different groups according to their respective levels of development (sometimes assumed on the basis of age). The researcher then compares peers or 'cohorts' as they successively reach a given age or point in development. This allows one to determine, in some cases, whether the observed changes are due to age, to cultural or historical factors, or a combination of both (Achenbach 1978: 101), since cultural or historical factors will be exhibited as differences between different cohorts at the same point in development. Such a method could be useful, for example, in exploring the relationship between acquisition and language change.

Although the observations in a longitudinal design ought to be made at regular intervals, one should not assume that by the same token development itself is regular. Bower (1974, for example) has examined many so-called repetitive processes in infant development, when a child apparently demonstrates an ability and then loses it, only to acquire it again later. Such is also the case for older children acquiring language, who must often 're-acquire' a form several times before mastery.

The requirements of large enough N, and frequent and regular intervals for moderately long observation sessions, will, if fulfilled, increase the validity of the data gathered. They will also, by the same token, add immeasurably to the inconvenience of research. Wells (1985) well described what one reviewer called the 'gory details' of his project (Golinkoff and Gordon 1987), and provided a horrendous-looking flow chart of the steps involved in just a single observation. Two solutions to part of the inconvenience problem which have been proposed are worth mentioning.

The recording methodology of Wells's Bristol project used a radio microphone timed to take twenty-four samples of 90 to 120 seconds each at 20-minute intervals between 9.00 a.m. and 6.00 p.m. An automatic timing mechanism switched on the radio receiver which was linked to a tape recorder. The battery-power supply was self-contained and kept in a sealed box inaccessible to the family volunteers. At the end of the day a research team member would come to the house and review the day's taping with the family, taking notes at that time concerning relevant features of the context in which the sampling occurred.

Clark (1976) also addressed the problem of making continuous recordings over long periods of time without having to record a great deal of silence and inactivity, or to have a diary at hand continually. She suspended omnidirectional microphones over the two rooms in which her subject spent the most time. The microphones recorded continuously onto a thirty-second loop, but when the child produced a novel utterance a switch could be turned by the caregiver which activated the tape recorder, capturing the utterance and a certain amount of preceding conversation. Attached to the switch was a long lead and another microphone into which the mother could whisper relevant information and an interpretation; this was recorded without delay onto a second track. The tape would run for another thirty seconds after the switch was turned off. This technique was supplemented with intermittently made recordings on a portable machine, sometimes while the mother was recording too, which could serve as a check on her 'switching' on and off. In this manner Clark was able to gather approximately thirty hours of data per week for a total of two-and-a-half years.

Of course, if novel utterances are the only stimulus for activating the tape recorder, then it is possible for the researcher to miss subtle changes in the child's language. Nowadays, the technology is available to activate recording equipment automatically simply by voice command. If such equipment, installed with manual override, could be developed and utilized, we would have a nearly ideal solution for gathering large amounts of longitudinal, naturalistic data at maximum frequencies, without having to make arbitrary decisions about either frequency or duration, or struggling too much to elicit data in an appropriately broad array of situations, and without having to fret too much about the effects on the subject(s) of an additional observer.

Wagner (1985) used mini-microphone transmitters to record several children over the course of a single day. Although one can be less sure of the representativeness of a single sample of this duration, there are advantages such as the amount of data (11,700 to over 37,000 utterances), and one can measure speaking versus silent time, actual versus potential speech, and listening time, among other things.

Related to the issue of longevity of a study is a problem which is difficult to circumvent. As Wells pointed out, the field of CLR continues to develop during the course of longitudinal data collection. The questions one had planned the study to answer may have become less important, or have already been answered, by the time the research project is complete (1985: 2). Since, however, one wishes CLR to progress, there is little that can be done about such a problem.

On the nature of the observer in data collection

The relationship between the observer and the subject of observation could profoundly affect the entire research process. There are essentially two aspects to this problem. One is the degree to which a given observer will introduce bias into the recording process, and this has already been touched upon; the other is the extent to which an observer may actually alter the communicative context in such a way that the data obtained will be unrepresentative. This is sometimes called the 'Observer's Paradox' – 'we want to observe how people talk when they are not being observed' (Labov 1971: 461).

Concerning the first aspect, the primary choice one must make is between a professional or caregiving observer/recorder, although sometimes one is both. While this choice can be superseded to an extent by using a neutral mechanical recording device, this of course merely postpones the introduction of human biases. Wells felt that comparisons of 'observer present' conditions with those in which the investigator comes after the observation period to fill in the context of audiotaped data do not clearly indicate the superiority of either (1985: 44).

Reliability studies of various sorts help to control, or at least mitigate, biases in the observation process. These generally require more than one observer or coder, and a sampling of their records to determine the degree to which there are differences. Yet, as Wells (1985) has noted, in studies of normal children reliability scores as low as 80 per cent have sometimes been reported; these are really distressfully low (see chapter 6 on measurement).

A type of observational bias may be introduced if for some reason in the course of the investigation there is a change in the observer. As Fassnacht put it, 'a ruler which constantly changes its length is of only limited value' (1982: 44). Nevertheless, consistency in this regard has not been a feature of instruments used in the social sciences, and the same may be true of CLR. Multiple members of a research team may be engaged in the process of observation and/or analysis of different children whose measurements will be combined, especially with large-scale research projects. Also, the same observer from day to day may be a source of inconsistency due to boredom, fatigue, habituation, learning, and other factors (Fassnacht 1982: 44). All of these are problems which may influence the observation process, although not necesarily the reality which one is trying to represent. For example, a parent may record that a child said 'I go with Mommy', when in fact the child actually said [a dow na mami]. 'I go with Mommy' may very well be the appropriate interpretation, but the interpretation itself is an element of observer bias which might lead to the erroneous conclusion that the child has acquired a specific preposition rather than just, say, a 'generic' prepositionlike particle.

Similarly, when a child is at the one-word stage, observers often supply 'meaning intentions' which may be dubious in their justification (Wells 1985: 88), a problem which also arises during coding. Olney and Scholnick (1978) demonstrated that presenting a deliberate mismatch between the visual context and the single-word utterances of one-year-olds impedes the observer's ability to identify the word. Videotaping may formalize our biases towards providing interpretations dependent upon immediate context, although these may not always reflect the child's intention. The real issue here is the extent to which the observer introduces bias into the recording process by recording first-order data, or data of a more abstract order. The distinction cannot always be made.

The degree to which the observer actually affects the type of data generated by the subjects determines the nature of the first-order 'facts' to be recorded. Most researchers agree that observers do affect data; they do not all agree on how. Very young children might try to establish contact with the observer, so some feel that young subjects should not be aware of observation (Schloon 1976, cited by Oksaar 1983: 54). However, hiding the observer behind a one-way screen or some other device means that subjects are likely to be in an abnormal environment (Fassnacht 1982: 183). Randall (1976) found social class differences in the degree to which an observer affects the interaction, noting that working-class (versus middle-class) mothers verbalized more to their infants when they were not aware of being observed. Wells found that expansions occurred with significant frequency only when a stranger was present at the mother–child interactions, suggesting that expansions function primarily to provide a gloss for the benefit of the non-caregiver (1980: 46).

Renne, Dowrick and Wasek wrote that, although they believed children tend to adjust relatively rapidly to the presence of observational devices, there are four ways in which the observation process might distort the behaviors one is trying to observe. First, as Schaerlaekens (1973) has also mentioned, there may be a change in the rate of the behavior. Second, there may be a change in the magnitude or the duration. Third, behaviors may appear which in some way or other impede those one wishes to observe. Finally, new, non-representative behaviors (e.g., expansions) might be introduced (Renne, Dowrick and Wasek 1983: 13–17).

As a type of model for the observation process which seeks to minimize observer effects, we can turn to psychoanalytic research. In addition to sharing a common origin in medicine with child development, it is epistemologically similar to CLR. For instance, researchers in both fields aim to understand certain aspects of the inner life, whether psychic or semantic, but cannot view these directly and so must make inferences from observed behaviors. In addition, the subject's social and interactive life are assumed to play a (sometimes major) role in shaping the reality one wishes to observe. Consequently, both fields face similar crises when it comes to identifying themselves as 'scientific' or not, and both face the same kinds of decisions about the degree to which the observer is or should be a participant in the situation being observed.

Margaret Mahler, a renowned psychoanalytic researcher, has long been committed to the direct observation of children as a means of understanding the processes which underlie 'overt' behavior (Kaplan 1978: 5). Her insights into and descriptions of her own research are applicable in many ways to CLR. She felt strongly, for example, that the interaction between observers and participants (both children and mothers) must be kept at a minimum. Doing so would help keep mother–child interactions as natural as possible, would allow mothers to relax if they perceived that they were in a non-authoritative atmosphere, and, furthermore, would avoid development of transference relationships to workers, which might be disruptive to the functioning of the dyads. For instance, mothers would sometimes try to solicit advice from the 'expert' observers, which was detrimental to research aims (Mahler, Pine and Bergman 1975: 32–3).

Mahler also believed that, especially in the earliest years, a child's kinesthetic and motor pathways are central to expression long before language develops. Because the behaviors expressed are end-products of inner states, the inner states themselves can be inferred, but only with a good degree of certainty through 'multiple, repeated and consensually validated observations and inferences' (Mahler et al. 1975: 15). This suggests that, just as a single-subject research design creates uncertainty, so does a design involving a single observer. Indeed, Mahler's research seems always to utilize two or more observers in addition to a camera.

An increase in the number of observers in addition to mechanical recording equipment, then, increases consensual validity. Observers may be differentiated according to setting: mother at home, but 'neutral' obervers in a laboratory setting, and so on. The degree to which equipment and observers may be discreet and unobtrusive, without being deceptive, is dependent upon arrangement of the research setting itself, an issue which directly affects efficacy of data collection. Further discussions of multiple observers and matters of their agreement can be found in the next chapter.

The research setting

Psychoanalytic research also favors naturalistic settings, a trend making its way into CLR. Many people criticize this preference, arguing that so-called contrived settings share many important features with so-called natural settings, and that, because of the possible presence of so many 'irrelevancies' in the natural context, one should make very sure that the behavior of focus really cannot be elicited any other way (Summerfield 1983: 9–10). This is a curious argument, putting naturalistic rather than experimental and other contrived forms of observation 'in the dock', so to speak. As noted previously, reflection on the history of the scientific disciplines reveals that observation must precede experimentation, just as the careful diary records of Charles Darwin preceded other forms of scientific observation (Fassnacht 1982: 181).

Given then that one need not justify the choice of naturalistic setting, if for no other reason than that we cannot really entirely assess the differences between it and experimental observation, there are two alternatives of procedure. Either the researchers must enter the environment of the subjects, or they must bring the subjects into an environment which will allow data to emerge that one hopes are representative of natural behavior.

Mahler et al. quipped that, although they did not go so far as to build a house for subjects to live in, they did develop a environment which was almost an extension of the home, and which they felt positively effected relevant data. This was accomplished by the construction of large infant and toddler play areas, adjacent to a pre-school, equipped with toys and the other usual paraphernalia, but also with comfortable furniture where caregivers (in this case mothers) cold sit and read, chat, have coffee, or simply watch their children play. 'Teachers' were researchers or assistants, although it was made clear that the mothers were to maintain their caregiving role. Observation was situated in hidden areas, but mothers knew that they and their children were being observed. A reduction in nursery-school tuition was offered as an incentive for participation in the research, although after a while word of mouth that the center was a relaxing and enjoyable place to bring young children soon filled any vacancies. The subjects were therefore self-selected although there was an initial screening to ensure that they were all normal – but the researchers did not feel that this would make much difference (see chapter 4).

The setting itself, both its arrangement and its ambience, influenced the data which were elicited in two ways. First, it had an effect on the content and quality of what was observed. The original rooms used in the research had toddler bathrooms and diaper-changing areas which were fairly accessible to observation, and this allowed researchers to observe specific interactions during toileting and diapering which were important to their particular topic (the individuation process). When they changed settings by moving into larger rooms, they could no longer observe these particular interactions, and thus lost a great deal of potentially relevant data.

The setting also affected the quality of the data. In general, the environment was designed to allow observers opportunity for repeated viewing of events and situations of concern in a setting which was semi-standardized and which allowed for the type of validation the researchers sought. Additionally, it was 'quasi-experimental' in that it allowed them to observe the very phenomenon which was their focus, specifically separation experiences (Mahler et al. 1985: 18–27).

Clearly, the setting influenced the degree of involvement between participants and observers. First, researchers established the principle that observers were not to interfere at all in the observed events, so that data might be collected which were as natural as possible. A solid partition was set up in the room, which allowed for researchers to observe what happened when children could not see their mothers, but this created a tendency for mothers to relinquish caregiving responsibilities whenever they could not see their children. Observers were thereby forced into direct caregiving activities they had wanted to avoid. The problem was solved by replacing the solid partition with a lower, slotted one through which children and mothers could view one another. After that, researchers were able to relax their 'no interference' rule in order to be able to observe, for example, the children's responses to outsiders (Mahler et al. 1975: 32–3). This then became a part of the data record available for comparative analysis.

Because of the similarities between psychoanalytic research problems and those in CLR, with the roles of interaction and intention being crucial to each field, the setting developed by Mahler and her colleagues serves as a good model. Aspects of a standardized setting can be manipulated in various ways in order for researchers to try to elicit explicit structures or content in a quasi-experimental manner. For example, in CLR one might remove an object that had previously been in the setting in order to try to elicit utterances concerning object permanence. The naturalness of interactions can also be enhanced when studies and settings have longevity, as Mahler's did. After several years, there are sufficient data for longitudinal analyses of individual children and peers, complementary cross-sectional studies, and time-lag analyses as well. This makes it less likely that any one researcher will produce a multitude of small studies, all based on different data and methods, but the precluding of such 'in and out' approaches to research can only benefit the field as a whole. One benefit it will provide is to make CLR graduate work more an apprenticeship, where students experience direct involvement with every phase of research in an ongoing study, allowing them the opportunity even to suggest (and try) changes in the design where they perceive a need for them.

6 The Organization and Analysis of Data

The setting has been designed to allow for a certain degree of standardization within a relaxing, naturalistic environment. An ample number of subjects have been selected, and the research process has been functioning for several weeks or months. The unblinking eyes of the videocamera have taken in hundreds of hours of data supplemented by reams of mothers' diary pages and observers' notes. The time at last arrives to begin a formal analysis of the data, requiring that they be organized first – a process which may hinder or enhance the analytic procedures. Looked at another way, the data have already passed through a selective filter during the collection phase; it remains for them to be passed through a still finer sieve.

The organization process will profoundly change what Bloom has referred to as the 'distance' between the original setting and the final analysis, depending upon how many stages are involved in the further structuring of data. Organization is not of course neutral to the analytic process, but for ease of discussion it will be treated as a separate step. Two sub-routines are involved: transcription, which is an optional process, and coding, which is obligatory but includes a range of possibilities considerably diverse in their complexity and purpose.

Transcription

Although it is possible to code videotaped or audiotaped data directly into categories of analysis, some degree of transcription is often performed. The purpose of this process is to synthesize all the data into a single record which represents both linguistic and non-linguistic events the transcriber deems relevant. This implies that the transcript is not as complete as the original records, but it is to be more informative and insightful for a given purpose. In fact, too much information renders a transcript difficult to read and evaluate (Ochs 1979: 44) so selectivity is an essential feature. Much interpretation therefore occurs during this process, and yet its reliability is seldom discussed (Wells 1985: 46–7).

Those with some experience in text analysis will have noted how the simplest conversation becomes extremely difficult to follow once it is presented in visual form, provided that the transcriber has faithfully represented the various behaviors which Chomsky described as the result of 'such grammatically irrelevant conditions as memory limitations, distractions, shifts of attention and interest, and errors (random or characteristic)' (1965: 3). These seemingly 'irrelevant' features are prominent in the transcript and may be considerably distracting, and yet they are decidedly important to the task of CLR for two reasons, making their retention as data essential. First, it is just these conditions with which the acquiring child must cope in his or her efforts to achieve communicative competence. The child will also produce many of these 'irrelevancies' himself or herself. This leads to the second point – that false starts, errors, breakdowns, and other limitations are windows onto the processes underlying language and its development. They may be important clues to transitional periods. For example, many children apparently stutter in the second year, most commonly when they are attempting utterances of much greater length than they had previously produced, or of greater semantic complexity. Valuable insights might have been lost, however, if during the selectivity process the transcriber had decided to filter out recycled syllables and words.

Of course, children's errors have long been considered acceptable data, and it is likely that some of the 'degenerate . . . quality' of the information children receive about language (Chomsky 1965: 31), motherese notwithstanding, may be linked to some of their own communicative weaknesses. While Chomsky assumed that the child must be able to differentiate sentences and non-sentences in order to devise the grammar (pp. 31–2), an extraordinary amount of language development occurs before children are clearly capable of such differentiation – development caught up in the negotiation of shared meanings more than in the testing of hypotheses about structure. Yet this is in many ways the most intriguing period of language acquisition, despite its being ill-suited to the linguist's interest in grammar writing.

Against this backdrop is the transcription made, and it subsequently supplants the original records as data for analysis. Ochs (1979: 44–5) remarked that researchers have been hindered by the lack of attention paid to transcription and its standardization. This has made it difficult not only to evaluate and use the data of others, but also to perceive the theoretical assumptions underlying the data, although, as Ochs herself went on to demonstrate, the latter is not entirely true. For example, side-by-side formats for adjacent turns are more theoretically appropriate for children between the ages of eighteen months and three years, since at this age they are more likely to link their utterances to their own prior talk than to the turn of another speaker (pp. 47–8). Whether this is a characteristic of the children at this stage, or of their interlocutors, is an interesting question.

The order in which one labels columns for verbal versus non-verbal behaviors can also be significant. Although non-verbal descriptions typically take up more space and one might be tempted to view the two types as distinct when they are in separate columns, nevertheless most agree that the immediate situational and behavioral context is crucial to interpretation of the child's language. If the non-verbal column is to the left of the verbal column, however, the coder may tend to give it more weight; the reverse is also true (Ochs 1979: 55–9).

Another way in which the organization of the transcript might affect analysis by highlighting certain pre-theoretical or theoretical assumptions is in the placement of the caregiver and child columns. The adult's utterances may be viewed as initiating, controlling, or constraining the child's if they are placed on the left; the child may be viewed as more competent if his or her column is on the left (Ochs 1979: 49–53).

Conventions regarding orthographic or phonetic transcriptions are also lacking, as is any standardization for the representation of non-segmental features. Orthographic representation is typical, and yet this may obscure certain aspects of development, such as the child's interpretation of contractions. If the transcriber writes 'could've' for example, this may be regarded by the adult as 'could have' but by the child as 'could of' (Fletcher 1985: 14–15). Evidence from young adults' written language would support the latter interpretation for many children.

Coding

An essential step in research according to canonical scientific method is the construction of hypotheses to account for the data at hand and any new data. This implies that something has emerged, or is expected to emerge, which needs to be accounted for. The coding process is essentially that aspect of analysis whereby something emerges. If the investigator feels he or she knows in advance what might emerge, data are typically fitted into *a priori* categories in an essentially deductive process. Other times, and increasingly in CLR, a more inductive approach is adopted which allows the categories to emerge *post priori* from the data. Hypotheses are not proposed in advance, but may be constructed abductively after the coding is accomplished; or the coding itself may constitute the analysis proper as a sort of exercise in abduction. Coding is the process of providing nomination for what is observed so that one can make judgments about whether observed phenomena are the same or different, and what the relationships are among the units or phenomena being observed. It clearly implies that an observational record consists of discrete units along the dimension of time or according to the nature of their content (Fassnacht 1982: 59). In CLR, units of content are most typical. While coding is frequently accomplished for the purposes of quantification, we will be treating this in a separate section, even though a relationship exists between categories of analysis and forms of quantification, especially in the extent to which units are interdependent or discrete.

Fassnacht described nominal systems as being verbal systems of representation with a more limited repertoire than ordinary language (1982: 91). Thus, in CLR (and linguistics in general) the record must be reduced to a system with decidedly fewer choices. Nominal systems are of two types: distinctive-feature or category systems. With the former, linguists are well familiar – distinctive-feature systems are composed of mutually compatible signs, meaning that a given phenomenon may receive more than one representation. These are logically open systems, and there is no guarantee that one has fully described any phenomenon, since one can always find more signs or features (Fassnacht 1982: 92–3). Technically, one can view distinctive features as a set of criteria, necessary but not necessarily sufficient, which allow one to classify, for example, an utterance as one thing or another – criteria such as one finds in Greenfield and Smith (1976). Although distinctive-feature systems are commonly used, albeit often in incomplete form, the features are not always as explicit as they need to be, being based on either hypotheses or convention (Fassnacht 1982: 92). Yet such operational procedures or justifications for the distinctive-feature system are especially critical if a researcher has employed 'coders' who need rules for assigning data to categories. This is because, although the categories may be ideal, actual speech is 'fuzzy'; this is especially true of semantic and functional categories (Wells 1985: 85–6 and 1982: 265–6), which are less discrete than is desirable for statistical analysis.

In the absence of justifying features or criteria, a nominal system may be a poor attempt at a true category system in which every phenomenon must fall into one category or another. The system is closed, the signs are not compatible, and a behavior is described completely (Fassnacht 1982: 95–7). Most CLR coding appears to be some sort of category system, although there are none which are complete, either in terms of being closed or in terms of providing a clear articulation of the relationships among the signs in the system. Again, discreteness is not always achieved in practice and many studies involve multiple coding schemes, not all of which are of the same type.

Kaplan defined coding as 'an explicit or implicit routine for characterizing perceptions or signals' (1984: 9). The soundness of one's conclusions depends in part on the degree to which routines are explicit, an issue which quite obviously also affects replicability. One's pre-theoretical and theoretical assumptions are boldly displayed in the choice of coding scheme. Some authors have used an admittedly 'eclectic' approach (Wells 1985, for example), drawn from a variety of theories and expectations; others may be strongly committed to specific theoretical positions.

Brown (1973) effectively summarized the central problem of coding schemes when he wrote that he could not simply 'code for grammatically significant features and put them on a computer' because he was never confident that he 'knew what the full coding should be' (p. 53). This statement also emphasizes the *a priori/post priori* contrast in coding styles, which to an extent reflects theoretical commitments. Debate in the literature occurs in this regard. To take a single example, Smith and Weist (1987) took issues with Rispoli and Bloom (1985) for the latter's use of emergent categories for the analysis of tense and aspect. Smith and Weist claimed that current theoretical models in linguistics, based in part on Aristotelian classification, are both explanatory and predictive in a wide variety of languages and hence were justified for use in child language analyses. They argued that the emergent categories were not well justified by data from children learning other languages, by independent use in the child's tense-aspect-modality system, or by major reorganization as children learn the categories in their target language. Rispoli and Bloom, reflecting a different pre-theoretical and theoretical base, felt that *a priori* categories beg the question of whether such 'categories translate into cognitive categories in any revealing way' (1985: 473). For Rispoli and Bloom, a linguistic theory which did not provide universals was inappropriate for use as a psychological theory. Wherever child language data could not be comfortably fit, in the researcher's judgment, into *a priori* schemes, emergent, *post priori* categorization has been defended. This is especially the case for functional and semantic analyses (see Duchan and Lund 1979).

Effective coding requires at least four parameters. First, one must have certain criteria for acquisition of a category if the end result is to determine that acquisition has occurred. Consequently, one must also have justification for these criteria (see below, pp. 88–9). One needs of course the categories themselves into which data will be coded, and finally, as noted above, there must be justification for these categories, in particular specifying the relationship between them and the interpretation one ultimately offers for one's results. It is in the area of categories and their justification that most problems relevant to coding occur; acquisition criteria tend to be considered aspects of measurement.

Coding is always a translation of concepts and observations into language, even if the concepts and observations are of a linguistic nature. Since the process is essentially one of translation, it renders our analyses vulnerable to what may be called 'restructuring' fallibilities common to all human communication. A given researcher may lose or distort relationships among concepts or data through the categorization, or actually recategorization, process (Kaplan 1984: 30), and it is these distortions one must take care to avoid. Bloom has written that one must beware of the risk, in classification, 'of losing the important variables and interactions that are not included in the . . . scheme' (1984a: 86). These especially are pitfalls of *a priori* schemes. *Post priori* coding, which sidesteps some of these difficulties, nevertheless creates its own monsters (pp. 80–1). And of course, the researcher may simply fail to communicate adequately to other researchers the nature of the categories.

One of the difficulties of *a priori* coding is that it sometimes imposes a classification too early. This can restrict hypothesis-testing by making it difficult to view the data in another light. Although coding is essentially a selection process, which is analytically distinct from description, Kaplan pointed out that, concretely, the two processes are indistinct. Descriptions are always selective to a certain extent, as well as tentative. They must be subject to revision, but cannot be if they are made 'without conscious thought', and, if they are so made, such descriptions will precede hypothesis-generating (Kaplan 1984: 149) and may therefore constrain it.

A second danger of *a priori* coding is its tendency to be dichotomous. One conceives, for example, of 'structures' versus 'functions' or 'semantic' versus 'syntactic' categories. Yet often such dichotomies are false, in the sense that they hinder us from viewing the two poles in their proper relation to each other. Dichotomous thinking tends to be the product of pre-theoretical processes, and may be culturally encouraged to a certain extent.

A major problem in CLR coding has been the imposition of the categories of analysis onto the data without the proper evidence that such categories have validity for young children (de Villiers and de Villiers 1974: 14). Categories such as parts of speech had to be abandoned by the Sterns because of their inadequacy for characterizing child speech (Greenfield and Smith 1976: 17–18). Such classification ignores the strong evidence in CLR literature that, when children learn to combine words, they are learning not parts of speech but relations among them (Bloom, Bitetti Capatides and Tackeff 1981: 408). This evidence, too, has come under fire, however. Matthews (1975) objected to the apparent confidence with which Brown (1973) wrote of 'prevalent relations', although Brown himself described numerous obstacles to the assignment of such categories; Howe (1976) has also been quite vocal about the problems of 'interpretive analysis'.

Some difficulties are not peculiar to *a priori* or *post priori* schemes, but plague all classification. Indeed, even *post priori* coding is not altogether novel – the categories which 'emerge' from the data for one researcher might be the same ones, perhaps with different names, that another scholar imposes. It is difficult to develop novel categories that are theoretically justified and at the same time sensitive to the data, and one may never know whether one's own research history becomes a set of blinkers, or an illuminating element, by which the same 'old' categories keep fitting or being fitted by new data because they are in fact correct. This is why systems of knowledge at the foundation rest essentially on faith, which is the only weapon one can yield against the uncertainty variable.

Another difficulty of coding in general but which may be more likely to occur under *post priori* schemes is inconsistency, either at the level of generality (Folger and Chapman 1978: 27), or with respect to a dichotomous framework. For example, a given use of language in children might seem to contain sub-categories, some of which are best characterized structurally, e.g., 'prepositional phrase', and others functionally, e.g. 'locative'. Since these two categories may not be mutually exclusive, and each may be an instance of the other, analysis will suffer from imprecision, a problem that occurs especially wherever formalism is disdained (Atkinson 1982: 228). In particular, some have felt that pragmatic categorization has had this difficulty, perhaps because its categories have not yet become entirely well established; but the argument can be made that, given the existence of pre-linguistic or non-linguistic coding systems (babies and animals certainly have these), cross-category difficulties may only indicate a failure of the apparently more consistent schemes to translate adequately from one classification system, e.g., that used by the child, to another, e.g., the 'adult' interpretation (cf. Kaplan 1984: 29). Rodgon (1977), for example, felt that scholars often tried to characterize the child's meaning in adult terms because of (1) a failure to conceptualize the world from the child's point of view, (2) the assumption that the child is trying to re-create an adult model, and (3) the assumption of shared mental capacity (and the extent of this) in the child and the adult.

In regard to selection of categories that are developmentally relevant, therefore, distinctions must always be well clarified by context, unequivocal, and non-ambiguous. Howe (1976) objected to interpretive analysis in part because she felt that the semantic categories proposed for children were an over-estimation of the child's cognitive capacity. Bloom, Bitetti Capatides and Tackeff challenged this view, claiming that not only were such categories 'derived from' rather than 'imposed upon' the data, but also that differences between the adult's and child's thinking are more quantitative than qualitative (1981: 407, 405–6). One presumes that the child's cognitive capacities must be similar enough to the adult's in structure that it is possible to explain the transitions in the developmental sequence, supporting the argument that semantically or cognitively based coding does have developmental relevance. Nevertheless, contextual cues, which have been heavily relied upon in this regard, may sometimes lead the researcher astray, as when the child performs an action irrelevant to the utterance, or refers to imagination rather than situation (Rodgon 1977).

Finally, one of the most difficult dilemmas to avoid is the circular one: proposing categories which the child must acquire as if he or she had already acquired them, thus begging the question of how the child learns what the appropriate categories are in the first place. The data a child receives must not be assumed to be 'preanalyzed' into grammatical units (Atkinson 1982: 231–2), unless we are willing to entertain and are unable to find evidence to reject a strong innateness hypothesis (which may be viewed merely as a hedge). One of the problems of so-called 'abstractionist' theories of concept formation, Atkinson maintained, is just this: the child acquiring the concept cannot 'compare instances' of it, in order to abstract similarities, unless he or she 'already knows that they are instances of a common concept', i.e., has already acquired the concept to be acquired (1982: 49). Circularity may also creep into analyses through measurement, as when children are categorized according to their performance on some variable which is not independent of the variable one wishes to measure.

In the short history of CLR, the ever-changing guiding principles and assumptions of the field have given rise to a multitude of different coding schemes. The early parts-of-speech approach reflected a belief in the primacy of form, as well as the assumption that language development was primarily the result of imitating the environment. Competent coding schemes which purported to capture internal aspects of speech were motivated by a belief in the ontogenetic recapitulation of phylogeny and, in general, the genetically oriented views of late nineteenth-century science (Oksaar 1983: 5–8). To this day, dichotomous thinking persists, although some scholars have been successful in coding from two perspectives (Greenfield and Smith 1976, for instance), suggesting that two schemes may not be contradictory; and dichotomies push their way into the field as a whole as long as both linguists and psychologists publish research which reflects, at times, extreme differences in perspectives. Schemes also reflect alternating beliefs, historically, that children either are or are not like 'miniature adults'; the prevailing view currently is that children are born with many innate abilities which make them more like adults than was believed in earlier decades, and our more complete and comprehensive coding systems reflect this idea.

In any coding system, one must keep in mind that individual differences among children may make it appear that the methodology lacks validity, when categories do not appear in the same ways across subjects. In part, this may reflect the degree of specificity of the scheme (Bloom, Bitetti Capatides and Tackeff 1981: 407). By the same token, some schemes are simply not valid. While the field could learn much from its failures, these are of course seldom revealed, since editors generally do not publish the research resulting from them. It would be provocative and edifying if now and then one would produce a volume of rejected papers written by some of the better-known scholars, with commentaries attached.

Clearly, as times change, so does the acceptability of coding procedures and systems. Where once a set of utterances may have fallen into apparently clear classes (pivot-open words, for example, or contentives-functors), they now no longer seem to, and we know it is not the character of the early utterances which has changed, but rather that new coding developments are evidence of a gradual, if not consistent, progress in our ability to learn about children's language acquisition.

Measurement in analysis

Once data are coded, the analysis may be complete if the intention was merely description. Most studies go on to interpret data further with the aid of measurement. At its most basic, an analysis may be grounded in descriptive statistics reporting only frequencies or percentages from which conclusions are drawn. If the analysis has been guided by one or more explicitly stated hypotheses, however, often the investigator turns to inferential statistical procedures. Much controversy is apparent over the relative validity of such procedures for certain types of analyses, and, in general, this aspect of analysis more than any other displays the division in the field between social scientists and others (Bennett-Kastor 1986a; see also chapter 7). Inferential statistics are associated especially with experimental approaches. Where the research has been contributed by linguists, whose training (at least in the United

States) has not typically included statistics, descriptive measures tend to be utilized, along with a preference for longitudinal, naturalistic data for which one cannot properly use multiple regression analyses since the assumption of independence among observations is violated (Scarborough, Wyckoff and Davidson 1986: 395). The controversy is not just methodological in nature, but also theoretical, hingeing on the degree to which one views language behavior as regulated by measurable probabilities of various sorts, by causal variables, or by features which are somewhat more elusive. Thus, the dominant generative framework of linguistics would neither call for nor lend itself to inferential statistics, even though complex data might thereby be reduced to much more 'manageable' levels (Woods, Fletcher and Hughes 1986: 1–2).

Types and functions of measurement

Measurement, like coding, is one of many forms of instrumentation used to obtain understanding. Kaplan has reminded us that language itself is also 'an instrument of inquiry' (1984: 137), and in linguistic study it may be a confounding one, since the same instrument is used both to frame what we measure and to be measured itself. New units of measurement are often devised as a way of defining new concepts or of objectifying, in some sense, observed phenomena.

The quantities used in the measurement of language differ according to the units one has chosen to isolate and categorize. The chosen unit can be measured in terms of frequency, duration, intensity, or some measure of the behavior as a whole (Fassnacht 1982: 115). The first is relatively clear-cut; the next two, in the case of language, are of somewhat dubious value, except in the extent to which a unit persists developmentally, in the case of duration. The last is the least clear but is typically the unit selected for measurement, assuming that measures such as 'range of semantic functions' or 'morpho-logical complexity', for example, represent measures of whole behaviors. Many of the categories or scales used in CLR are nominal, which lend themselves to few inferential and virtually no parametric statistical analyses. 'Scores', readily used in an inferential study, are not often obtained. Suffice it to say that the problem of what to measure and how to measure is a thorny one.

Wittgenstein wrote that one of the defining qualities of the act of measurement is constancy (1954: 242). A given measure becomes reliable in the course of the practice of a field, and then becomes part of its characteristic arsenal of instrumentation, but only for a particular field. In CLR, the appropriate instruments are still being developed. This task is complex, and consequently analyses are sometimes adopted wholesale by subsequent researchers not because they are thoroughly justified epistemologically or theoretically, but because it is convenient to do so. Although this lends a type of consistency to the field in so far as such analyses then become justified praxically, in time such practices are usually challenged either by problems which arise within the praxical framework (e.g., MLU and the difficulties of calculating it) or external to it (e.g., a shift in theoretical perspective, as when an interactionist or cognitive framework comes into dominance and demands measures more relevant than those from the previously dominant framework).

What is the function of measurement in CLR? Typically, it exists for the purposes of making comparisons across children of aspects of their language, in order to provide evidence for development (Prideaux 1985: 60–3), or simply for describing the nature of language use in children, or apparently for validating the measure itself. At least two measures are usually provided in any sutdy, corresponding to IV and DV, although these are often only implicitly defined. The question of what measures for each purpose are both relevant and valid is of course separate from the question of what measures are typically utilized, since CLR is a relatively new field, but it is helpful to look at the usual measures with an eye to the ultimate goals of CLR and the purposes of the act of measurement itself.

In CLR, as in all fields, measurement is prone to uncertainty. Some uncertainty stems from the inability to define a measure precisely, other uncertainty is the result of trying to apply the measure, and yet another type comes in the attempt to generalize or otherwise interpret the measurement. Each of these sources of uncertainty can be identified with a number of the typical measures used in CLR.

Ages and stages

Chronological age is certainly a common and relatively easy, if crude, form of measurement, especially used as an IV. While there is little difficulty in defining it, and one would think little difficulty in applying (i.e., assessing) it, two major disadvantages are associated with age. First, one must decide what the relevant intervals are against which development will be measured. Second, the problem of diversity in development (Prideaux 1985: 61–3) will compound the arbitrariness problem in distinguishing intervals. Obviously the two issues are interwoven, since if age were an accurate, necessary, and non-neutral predictor of development, it would be easier to know if children should be divided into groups according to one-year, six-month, or twelve-week intervals. Nevertheless, the use of age as an IV is the most frequently encountered single measure in CLR, as in a number of disciplines; and although it may appear to be theoretically neutral, it does in fact reflect a developmentally oriented perspective allied with non-behaviorist, non-structuralist, and naturalistic approaches.

A related type of measure is the 'stage' or 'level', which may either implicity or explicitly be associated with age, or used as an alternative IV. Regardless of their origin in either inductive or deductive processes, stages are for the most part, in Wells's words, a 'descriptive convenience imposed upon a continuous developmental process' (1985: 225). Wells used the term 'level' for what appeared in his data as groups of items which were co-emergent in acquisition, and at least weakly ordered with respect to one another (p. 201). Brown (1973) is the most common reference for the use of 'stage' in CLR; he admitted to their being arbitrary divisions rather than 'true' stages, and, although they are based on mean length of utterance (MLU), it is unclear why they should correspond to the various developments which are said to occur with each – roles and relations within a simple sentence (Stage I), modulations of meaning (Stage II), and modality of the simple sentence (Stage III) – since these developments could just as well be interpreted to occur at different stages (Matthews 1975: 323ff). Nevertheless, 'stage' as applied by Brown (1973) is widely used, so much so that it occurs without reference. Since this is so, and since these stages are determined on the basis of MLU (in morphemes, or MLUm), it is essential in the assessment of analysis in CLR to scrutinize MLUm more closely.

MLU

MLU, whether used as proposed by Brown as MLUm or in less sophisticated form as average words per utterance, has been used as both IV and DV. As the former, it is certainly less neutral developmentally than age, and may be causally or otherwise linked to age and other aspects of communicative development. While some (e.g., Dale 1980) have found that, once age is partialled out, MLU is not statistically related to number of pragmatic functions expressed, and others (Klee and Fitzgerald 1985) found it poorly correlated with either age or other measures of grammatical development, at least some research (Miller and Chapman 1981) has shown strong positive correlations of MLU with age. MLU is also used on occasion as a DV, where it is assumed to be a measure of grammatical complexity, especially when morphemes rather than words are calculated. Brown has pointed out, however, that beyond a certain point (MLUm 4.00), it no longer reflects grammatical development, since the length and content of a child's utterances come to depend more on factors inherent in the interaction (1973: 54). In fact, it has not yet been adequately justified empirically as an index beyond Stage II (MLUm 2.50), or even earlier (Klee and Fitzgerald 1985).

MLU reflects a theoretical orientation that respects the primacy of linguistic development for its own sake. Throughout *A First Language*, Brown revealed a generativist bent which was, nevertheless, not always acknowledged (Crystal 1974b). MLU is not a measure which means to subjugate communicative development to cognitive, social, or other types, and certainly not even to chronological development, although it apparently correlates with age somewhat for three-year-olds (Conant 1987). In this sense, MLU is the measure which best represents the Chomskyan view that the linguistic system is qualitatively different in complexity from other systems underlying human behavior, and hence a separate mental capacity.

Although MLU has the distinct advantage of having appeared throughout the literature for over a decade (Fletcher 1985: 46), several disadvantages are associated with it, in its definition, application, and interpretation. The first problem is that of defining for the child the relevant unit; this is not always easy for adult speech (e.g., 'gonna', 'wanna'), especially in languages with myriad suppletive and irregular forms, not to mention the problems posed by compounds, idioms, and prefabricated routines (Crystal 1974b: 297–8). As a case in point, Vihman, Macken, Miller, Simmons, and Miller (1985), in their study of the transition from babbling to speech, reported the considerable methodological efforts they made just to define 'word' for a given child – a necessary prerequisite to pinpointing the period they wished to study.

Second, although Brown offered guidelines and justifications for ways of calculating utterance length, the use of 'morpheme' specifically is not well reasoned (as opposed to some other unit), and it must be assumed that individual children will present different manifestations of the grammatical system which must then be assessed on a case-by-case basis. Crystal, for instance, wondered how to determine even what an 'utterance' is, as the guidelines require that one count 100 utterances (1974b: 296). This is to say nothing of research on children acquiring other languages which, as Brown noted, may have morphological systems which operate so differently from English that increase in length does not indicate increase in complexity and, therefore, development. Dromi and Berman reported that such was the case in the highly synthetic Hebrew language. MLU was deemed inappropriate not just for Hebrew, but probably for highly inflected languages in general, for which MLU values will be inflated (Dromi and Berman 1982: 404). Crystal, too, felt that Brown's rules were rather 'English-oriented'.

Another objection to MLU is a practical one. Extensive analysis is required for one to obtain the score – analysis both of the child's grammatical system and, to discover this, of the meaning of each utterance (Prideaux 1985: 62–3). Since what a morpheme is can be determined only on the basis of a well-developed grammar for the child, how can MLU be used *a priori* as a measure of grammatical development (Arlman-Rupp, van Niekirk de Haan and van de Sandt-Koenderman 1976)? If MLU is to be used as an IV, then one must still analyze and measure something else; as a DV, it is quite unsatisfying, since it really is unclear just what it measures. Perhaps these are the main reasons that MLU is not often used as a single measure in CLR, despite its 'pure' linguistic character, but tends to be used in combination with other measures.

Although Brown's rules require the use of 100 utterances satisfying certain criteria (1973: 54), in some cases there will be children who simply will not produce this many. In very young children, e.g., those not yet combining morphemes and/or those uttering 'Gestalt-like', apparently unanalyzed sequences, MLU may simply be inappropriate. Crystal questioned why, in the selection of the utterances, the first page of transcript needs to be disregarded any more than any other page (1974b: 295); certainly this reduces still more what at times may already be a limited corpus. And which is more reasonable, to take 100 consecutive utterances, or every fifth of 500 utterances, since data from the latter will presumably be more independent (Woods et al. 1986: 104–5)?

To finish the litany of complaints against MLU we should add that it is also difficult to justify theoretically and to maintain in practice the assumption that semantic and grammatical complexity are separable (Wells 1985: 357). Furthermore, the variability in MLU for all levels of development is apparently much greater than Brown anticipated (pp. 335–40). Klee and Fitzgerald found that the standard error may be as much as three stages, in addition to the measure's poor predictability of either age or other measures of grammatical development such as those associated with LARSP (see p. 92). Crystal found in general that Brown's rules for calculating MLU were too inexplicit to be helpful – what should the role of prosody be in determining utterance or other unit boundaries, for example? Why was no reliability reported for agreement among analysts? How should one actually deal with doubtful transcriptions? What is an 'exact repetition'? A 'filler'? Worst of all, the justification for using MLU is that age is too variably related to rate of development, and yet, wrote Crystal, 'similar results . . . can be obtained without having to use a sampling superstructure which has creaky linguistic foundations' (1974b: 300).

Alternatives to MLU

Type-token ratios

Myriad other measures have been used either to supplement or to replace MLU altogether; the majority of published work in CLR apparently does not rely solely on Brown's measure (see chapter 7). One fairly simple measure which, however, is also seldom used as the sole assessment tool is the type-token ratio (TTR). Especially in research involving children with communicative disabilities it is commonly reported, although it occasionally appears as well in studies of normal children, both as an input variable and as a child-production variable. The assumption of TTRs is that they reflect lexical diversity. Presumably, larger TTRs indicate less repetitive vocabulary usage, and this measure is supposed to be independent of sample size. Templin (1957) reported fairly equivalent TTRs for subjects ranging in age from three to eight, even though eight-year-olds used nearly twice as many different words in fifty utterances. This is somewhat surprising, and Richards (1987) claimed that such a conclusion was indicative of theoretical and methodological problems with the measure.

First, TTRs are in fact quite sensitive to sample-size variation. When calculated from a large sample, TTR will generally be smaller than the measure calculated on the basis of a smaller sample, since each additional word type comes closer to the limits of the child's productive lexicon. Second, the standardization of the corpus for number of utterances will cause TTR to decrease with age, as the same number of utterances by older children will consist of more tokens and, consequently, a smaller TTR. Richards demonstrated that even in a sample from Chomsky TTR fell as more tokens were included! For these two reasons, TTR's frequent use as a clinical tool is premature. Norms have yet to be established.

TTR may also be constrained considerably by context. Presumably, certain conversational situations might allow for more far-ranging topics shifts which would in turn result in more tokens and/or types. Thus, TTR would vary depending upon how the samples on which it was based were obtained and whether they all represented similar situations.

Richards believed that one should divide the data into closed and open lexical classes before calculating TTR. Although both are affected by sample size, open-class words will result in higher TTRs than will closed items. The measure he recommended was to use at least 400 tokens in order to minimize the effect of sample size, and use a logarithm of number of tokens to obtain a more linear relationship between TTR and sample. Alternatively, one could use the measure reported in Carroll (1964: 54), as follows:

$$\frac{n \text{ types}}{\sqrt{2n \text{ tokens}}}$$

Acquisition criteria

Another approach to measurement, usually for DVs, is establishment of various criteria for acquisition of grammatical and other distinctions, and their justifications. Such measures tend to be fairly linguistic in their orientation, although they need not be. Brown (1973), in determining order of acquisition, used the criterion of 90 per cent use in obligatory contexts. In the area of phonology, a criterion of seven out of ten correct has been used, for example by Edwards (1974), to determine phone discrimination. Yet Barton (1975) objected that this injects such a huge random error into the results as to render them uninterpretable: in 11.72 per cent of sessions, there might be seven correct by chance alone. Wells felt that even Brown's criterion level was inadequate. It might not be appropriate across dialects, for instance, nor are items which one wishes to measure always obligatory. Adjusting the percentage for criterion for each category, on the other hand, is problematic because of the differential probability of occurrence of items in particular domains (e.g., nominals versus verbals). Also, the very low frequencies of some categories, even in adult speech, pose measurement problems. His solution was to substitute the notion of 'emergence' of an item, defined as the first instance of a category followed by successive usage generalizable across subjects, even though some categories are slow to spread into all relevant contexts (Wells 1985: 130–3). In this manner, Wells was able to see 'clusters' of emergent categories and to use these for determining 'levels' in the acquisition process which were at least somewhat less arbitrary than Brown's stages.

Miscellaneous measures

Pragmatic functions are apparently measurable too, though agreement may not be as high as for structural features, and these offer information about development that is neither provided by, nor related to, MLU (Dale 1980). The semantic functions measured by Greenfield and Smith (1976) (familiar also in Bloom's and Brown's research and some from Fillmore's case-grammar), such as 'agent', 'locative', and 'modification of an event', can be measured in terms of frequency, range, or emergence-acquisition criteria, as can more functional measures, whether as narrow as the illocutionary approaches of Dore and Bates or as general as Haliday's 'interactional', 'regulatory', or 'imaginative' functions. These indicate a continuing trend in CLR to delve beneath structural features of a child's language in order to assess its character as a vital part of the child's developing social and cognitive life. The ideal measures would in fact not be based on any unitary concept but would adequately represent all the dimensions of language which develop in concert or in parallel, and give due weight to each (Wells 1985: 125). The diversity of measurement represents, then, not just theoretical dichotomies in CLR, but also the nature of language and its use.

One general problem with this diversity is finding compatible measures. If we are to conceive of development as occurring in some way in 'stages', it is important to remember that children are neither necessarily at the same stage of development for each skill acquired (Corrigan 1978: 174), nor should 'stage' according to one measure necessarily correlate with 'stage' as defined by another. This is in part because of the arbitrariness of divisions, but it also reveals how much we have yet to learn about the intricacies of linguistic sub-systems. Furthermore, the external criteria we may establish to justify and apply measures may themselves be mutually incompatible. In Wells's case, for example, criteria of 'saliency' of an item and 'clear ordering' of emergence were frequently not compatible (1985: 279).

Computer analysis

Computers are being called upon as tools of analysis with increasing frequency. They have been a mixed blessing, introducing almost as many difficulties as they have solved. Wells cautioned that, if the linguist and the programmer do not work carefully together from the very earliest point, the time and effort expended may grow 'out of all proportion to the nature of the original problem' (1985: 110). By the same token, the use of computers to code and analyze data can force one into a degree of explicitness to which one might not otherwise aspire. This can be of immense benefit, although humans and computers may do things in ways which are at times at odds. For example, computers prefer fixed formats in which the same column always contains the same information; humans can be quite comfortable with freer formats (Wells 1985: 55).

Statistical packages are readily available for both mainframe and personal computers. In addition, programs are available for the analysis of data prior to any statistical processing. Four of these are known as DSA, LINGQUEST, SALT, and LARSP. The use of these and other such programs also represents something of a dichotomy in the field, in this case between practitioners allied with communicative disorders and others not so allied. This is not to say that, for example, linguists have not developed programs for language analysis in general, but rather that those which have been marketed and utilized most by CLR practitioners are associated with research in language disability. One reason for this may be that, at least for linguists, it is often felt that there is simply no substitute for human intuition, the workings of which have not been successfully mechanized, even though it is an inefficient system.

DSA

Developmental Sentence Analysis, including the Developmental Sentence Score (DSS), is a procedure developed by Laura Lee of Northwestern University (Lee and Canter 1971; Lee 1966; 1974) but now available as a program (Computerized Programming by Steven H. Long 1986, which also includes LARSP). Lee, a speech pathologist, was primarily concerned with assessment. The procedure provides for analysis of the occurrence of noun modifiers, pronouns, main and secondary verbs, negatives, conjunctions, interrogative reversals, and WH-questions, assigning a weight to each. The child receives a single score – the DSS – which is, however, not apparently well correlated with any other measures. In a study of the last 50 utterances in the corpora of 20 children, for example, Lee (1974) displayed a higher DSS for Stage I (MLU $\geq$ 1.99) than for Stage II (MLU 2.00–2.49) in children aged 2;0 to 2;5, but DSS was higher at Stage II for children ages 2;6 o 2;11. Its relationship to either age or MLU does not appear to be linear. Another disadvantage of the measure is its insensitivity to dialectal differences. Only 'complete' utterances are scored, but utterances complete by the standards of a dialect which deleted certain copulas, no matter how complex, would not be counted. Only intelligible and 'different' (no repetitions of self- or other) utterances may be used; the preferred sample size is 100 consecutive utterances, although 50 may be used. Some time is devoted in Lee (1974) to problems of separating utterances for the DSS or for the accompanying DST ('Developmental Sentence Types') designed to handle so-called 'pre-utterances'. In the end, the child is reduced to a single score which, although clinically practical, is rather unsatisfying for research purposes.

LINGQUEST

LINGQUEST is actually comprised of two programs – one for morphology and syntax, and one for phonological analysis. Using a 50 to 100 utterance sample for which an 'expanded form', as well as the actual utterance, is entered and marked for nouns, some verbs, and participles, the computer will execute an analysis of form, structure, lexicon, and tense resulting in various quantitative measures including MLU. For the form analysis the program reports number of 'correct' instances of use, number of opportunities for occurrence, percentage of correct usages, and number and types of 'errors' for eight categories of form – nouns, verbs, modifiers, prepositions, conjunctions, negation, interjections, WH-question words – comprising 81 sub-categories. Omissions are also automatically tabulated, and specific 'errors' are shown in a so-called 'substitution profile'. Structural analysis involves similar analyses for types of basic and complex sentences, questions, and noun phrases, verb phrases, and modifier phrases. The lexical analysis basically provides a type-token ratio, and the verb-tense analysis operates on twelve verb 'tenses' (tense-aspect combinations), providing frequencies and/or percentages of opportunities for and actual uses of these.

The phonological analysis is based on a phonetically transcribed and entered corpus. The program will perform a phonemic analysis which includes an inventory with information on contrastivity and range of variability. Based on distinctive feature theory, a substitution profile is compiled which collapses phonemes into natural classes and provides ratios of correct/incorrect use for initial, medial, and final consonants and initial clusters, identifying features of incorrect use. Omissions are similarly analyzed, as are vowels. Although LINGQUEST would appear to be a powerful analytic tool, it is rarely referred to in the CLR literature.

SALT

The SALT (Systematic Analysis of Language Transcripts) program, developed by Miller and Chapman (1983), is similar to DSA but does not weight items. It provides frequency and percentage of utterance types per speaker for categories such as 'total', 'complete versus incomplete', and 'intelligible, partly intelligible, and unintelligible'. Distributional summaries are based on utterance length in words and morphemes and the number of utterances of each length; word and morpheme summaries also appear as type-token ratio, MLU, classification into stage (Brown 1973), and the number of different root words and total words. Categories such as questions, negation, coordination, modal auxiliaries, 'semi'-auxiliaries (e.g., 'gonna', 'wanna') are included. One can also execute searches of various sorts and will be provided with, for example, a child's response to WH-questions together with the preceding and following utterances.

LARSP

The Language Assessment, Remediation, and Screening Procedure (LARSP) was developed by Crystal, Fletcher, and Garman (1976) (revised 1981). It responds to some of the shortcomings of DSA. Based on the grammar of Quirk, Greenbaum, Leech, and Svartik (1972), it provides an analysis of clause and phrase types which has been used primarily for assessment. It is designed in such a way that it takes into consideration the earliest 'proto-constructions' of children (Fletcher 1985: 74), and is more widely used in CLR than the other three programs.

Utterances from a sample of 30 minutes, which in normal children will usually result in 100 to 200 utterances (Crystal et al. 1976: 87), are classified according to categories labeled 'unanalyzed/problematic', 'responsive', or 'spontaneous', with frequencies provided. Responses are described according to frequency of stimulus type (question or other), and then repetitions, normal, and abnormal responses and their types. Spontaneous utterances provide for the primary analysis. Utterances are considered major or minor, the latter including routines of various sorts. Sentence-structure analysis of major utterances includes exclamatory types, commands, questions, and statements. Each of these is analyzed in more detail, particularly statements, for which is provided information on clause and phrase types, as well as some lexical analysis, especially of grammatical morphemes. Discourse elements are also considered, as in examples of connectivity. LARSP is not intended for phonological analysis, but aside from this it is one of the most comprehensive of the procedures, including as it does analyses of multiple linguistic levels.

Computer analysis of data is clearly the wave of the future and has revolutionized many fields. One does, however, pay a price for it. In particular, data must usually be prepared in a specific way for a given program, and the format required may be wholly incompatible with that required by another program. Such analyses therefore have the potential to limit the value of any single corpus and constrain in this manner the most productive uses of the data, which can, however, always be reformatted.

Reliability procedures

Another form of measurement which must be addressed, since it appears in nearly a quarter of published works in CLR, is the measure of reliability, especially between two or more analysts, of judgments involving categories of analysis. Especially when the measures being used are unfamiliar and/or the criteria somewhat inexplicit, researchers may adopt one of two strategies to better ensure reliability. One approach is to design the setting, frequency, duration, longevity, and other aspects of observation in such a way that unrepresentative behaviors would be unlikely to keep occurring. A second approach, less effective but important (although it should not replace the first), is the use of inter-observer reliability measures at various stages. Surprisingly, such measures are not used as often as one might hope. Typically, two or three people make a judgment about a transcription or categorization, and the number who agree on the classification becomes the numerator which, when divided by the number of persons making the judgment (the denominator), results in a ratio. Usually, agreement on individual items is not reported; rather, an overall score is given representing the average of all judgments.

While reliability measures certainly ought to be used, one must not become too complacent with relatively high scores, for the following reasons. High agreement is not necessarily the result of appropriate coding, but rather of the observers' all having the same biases, operating definitions, and expectations for categories (Bloom 1974a: 86). Second, overall reliability may mask strong disagreement over certain individual categories. Wells (1985) remarked that estimates of reliability may be quite different depending upon whether they were calculated as the proportion of utterances containing one or more disagreements (e.g., in analyses involving multiple codings of each utterance), or the number of disagreements as a proportion of total judgments. Wells used a combination of procedures, but this as not always detailed. A related problem is that it is necessary to state and justify a standard – at which the agreement is high enough for the analysis to be deemed reliable – and develop a procedure to be followed whenever agreement drops below the criterion. Unfortunately, neither standards nor ameliorating procedures are often reported.

An unusual but sometimes encountered variation of the reliability measure can be used when there is a single observer. In this case, the independent analyst will make the same analysis two or three times, then calculate agreement among his or her own successive judgments. Although this is better than nothing, it can be suspect, since single researchers may simply be repeatedly applying their own biases or other errors, and may learn to agree with themselves. Nevertheless, it is a useful tool for demonstrating to oneself the degree to which criteria for judgments need to be better operationally defined.

Statistical measurement

Thus far the discussion of measurement has proceeded without much assessment of its role in the sometimes dichotomous nature of CLR methodology. With the subject of statistical analysis, however, it is quite clear that the decision to engage in descriptive or inferential analyses is heavily influenced by the discipline of the researcher and the epistemological and theoretical principles to which he or she is committed. Although the use of inferential measures is nearly a hallmark of the social sciences, in the case of linguistics it is not common practice at all. Slightly under 40 per cent of a random sample of studies in CLR reported descriptive statistics only (or none at all); 80 per cent of linguists and other scholars associated with the humanities, as opposed to about 20 per cent of psychologists and other social scientists, utilized no inferential statistics. In contrast, only 16 per cent of linguists and humanities-allied practitioners in CLR utilized two or more inferential measures, compared to 46 per cent of psychologists and other social scientists (see chapter 7, which discusses methodological trends in more detail).

In part, this trend reflects the use of small N in studies by linguists; also the use of nominal categories and their frequencies, which do not lend themselves well to inferential analyses, plays a role. Nevertheless, even in the absence of assessments of the degree to which differences in data are significant, many scholars do not hesitate to make developmental claims.

The description-only trend practised by a number of linguists ultimately has a much deeper cause – namely, the theoretical orientation towards language, especially grammar, as a qualitatively different sort of behavioral phenomenon from others which researchers believe to be measurable. Where writing a grammar is at issue, mere probability is useless. Chomsky himself made his stand clear when he wrote that, although there has been great interest in 'statistical studies of language, they appear to have no direct relevance to the problem of determining or characterizing the set of grammatical utterances' (1957: 17).

Despite these views, use of inferential statistics appears to be increasing in CLR, even by linguists. While it is true that such measures can be and have been overused, more and more CLR practitioners are becoming aware that statistics do play a role in some linguistic analyses, and that developmental claims can be strengthened when larger numbers of subjects are used in combination, where appropriate, with even fairly elementary statistical procedures. These have nothing to do with probabilistic accounts of grammar, but rather with assessing the significance of change in variables such as MLU, number of functions, number of structural types, and so on with age or group. The two difficulties which still remain are that, at some point which is difficult to specify, fluctuation of such scores will no longer be developmentally relevant but instead sensitive to qualities of the interactional context; and researchers must still find ways to design essentially naturalistic, longitudinal studies which provide data that can be statistically treated. Concerning the first problem, Wells commented on how difficult it was to determine, for example, order of acquisition among later emerging items, since as the range of options increases, so does inter-subject variability in the use of the options (1985: 278). Statistical analysis might actually clarify such variability to an extent where probabilities become high, indicating that fluctuations can no longer be attributed to developmental effects. Nevertheless, regression analysis is not entirely appropriate for assessing behavioral measures of the quality and nature of family–child interactions (Wells 1985: 351–2).

In regard to the second difficulty, some studies have already been successful (e.g., Wells), and have demonstrated that there is not necessarily complete incompatibility between statistical analyses of data and naturalistic observation. As more and more of the relevant variables are understood, the possibility for inferential procedures to be routinely injected into such studies will increase.

One area where statistical measurement has been extensively utilized, and the appropriateness of various measures debated, is, as seen in chapter 1, in the area of environmental influences of various sorts on the language-development process. In addition to design issues in analyses of 'motherese' and its effects, the role of infants' early linguistic experience in their perception of phonemic contrasts has also been treated. Eilers, Gavin, and Oller (1982) tested discrimination of Spanish flapped versus trilled /r/, English inter-vocalic /s/ versus /z/, and Czech syllables /ža/ and /řa/ by infants with English and Spanish language backgrounds. After training trials with the syllables /ba/ and /da/ during which infants were reinforced for head-turning responses associated with a change in the stimulus, the subjects heard naturally (rather than synthetically) produced stimuli matched for duration, amplitude, fundamental frequency, and pitch contour. Eilers, Gavin and Oller claimed that their study eliminated earlier studies' confounding variables such as intrinsic difficulty or saliency of native versus non-native contrasts, and features of research design which were also confounding. They concluded that, since Spanish infants displayed statistically significant evidence of discrimination of all three contrasts and English infants of the English versus Czech contrasts, therefore not only does early linguistic experience affect perceptual discrimination, but available techniques are sensitive enough to detect performance differences.

However, MacKain (1982) outlined the conditions which would in fact have to be met before one could draw such a conclusion. Voice-onset times must match natural, not ideal, VOTs in the target languages, and these typically display considerable variability. 'Linguistic experience' must be adequately and clearly defined. For example, is it assumed that mere exposure to contrasts means 'experience' with them? Does sensitivity evidenced in a laboratory necessarily tell us anything about how infants really experience sounds in natural speech contexts? If so, one must assume that the infant has already accomplished (a) segmentation, (b) recognition of requirements of contrastivity, (c) recognition of the irrelevance of some types of redundancy, (d) recognition of contrastivity of some variation but (e) not of other variation, (f) assumption of comparability of previous and current experience, and (g) accounting for frequency of apparent contrasts (MacKain 1982: 534–5). For all these reasons, the author felt that it would be more productive to look indirectly at the possible effects of linguistic experience on, for example, babbling.

Oller and Eilers (1982) did just that, by examining babbling in twelve-month-old infants from English and Spanish backgrounds. Their study, which did not comprise the extensive statistical procedures used by Eilers, Gavin and Oller, resulted in the conclusion that, despite 'gross phonetic differences' between English and Spanish, the infants' babbling was similar, consisting primarily of consonant-vowel syllables with voiceless, unaspirated plosives. This would not support the conclusions drawn by Eilers, Gavin and Oller from their perceptually based experiments.

The work of Eilers, Gavin and Oller was in fact criticized, largely on statistical grounds, by Jusczyk, Shea, and Aslin (1984), who were puzzled by the conclusions. They claimed that bizarre statistical analysis was to blame for the odd results, where it would have been expected instead for Spanish infants to perform better on Spanish contrasts, English infants on English contrasts, and Czech infants on Czech contrasts. Since discriminatory performance for the infants on the three contrasts ranged from 52 per cent to 62 per cent and 50 per cent would be chance, how could such low scores achieve significance in only fourteen subjects? Jusczyk et al. claimed that the problems were, first, in the use of a so-called 'discriminative index' (DI) using the formula

$$DI = \frac{n \text{ correct responses or 'hits'} - n \text{ false positive responses}}{n \text{ possible hits}}$$

Jusczyk et al. felt that Eilers, Gavin and Oller should simply have used 'percentage correct' (PC) instead and also objected to the use of the z-test in place of the t-test (or other appropriate non-parametric test). Jusczyk et al. believed that DI generated more significant differences and thereby increased the likelihood of the authors' committing a Type I error to conclude falsely, as did Eilers, Gavin and Oller, that infants would discriminate a contrast. As regards the z-test, it requires that one know the population variance. Although Eilers, Gavin and Oller used a computer simulation of 10,000 pseudo-subjects, Jusczyk et al. felt that this program confused trials with subjects as the unit of analysis where independent observation of subjects was required. Had Eilers, Gavin and Oller used PC scores and a test such as Tukey-planned comparison of the means, it is unlikely, claimed Jusczyk et al., that results would have exceeded chance. Furthermore, there was a confounding variable in that only the Czech contrasts displayed the acoustic saliency of single syllable-initial position.

Eilers, Oller, Bull, and Gavin (1984) responded by reanalyzing their own data using PC versus DI and both t- and z-tests. They claimed that, in either case, the results were comparable, further arguing that not only is zm perfectly conventional, but the sample variance associated with t is actually often smaller than the population variance associated with z. Eilers, Oller, Bull and Gavin assured Jusczyk et al. that all observations for randomly responding infants in the Eilers, Gavin and Oller computer simulation were independent, justifying trial as the unit of analysis. Absolute levels of infant discriminatory performance may have been poor, but they were nevertheless significantly above chance whether measured by means of z or t-tests.

Besides, Jusczyk et al. miscalculated the DI for randomly responding infants. Thus do surprising results, countered Eilers, Oller, Bull and Gavin, not necessarily indicate methodological flaws.

Reviewing such debates about the proper use of statistical measures, one can sometimes understand why linguists have been hesitant to enter the fray. Views are gradually being altered, however; textbooks for statistics in linguistics have appeared (Woods, Fletcher and Hughes 1986, for example), and familiarity with such basic measures as ANOVA (analysis of variance), t-tests, X^2, and the Spearman rho and Pearson product-moment correlations will enhance the degree to which CLR practitioners from various disciplinary backgrounds can share each other's insights and make informed decisions about the role which statistics will play in their own research. The wide availability of statistical packages for the computer (such as those outlined in Woods et al. 1986), including Minitab and SPSS, will also contribute to increased use. In turn, the gap in training between linguists and social scientists should begin to close as the former recognize the value of having a basic understanding of inferential measures.

Obviously, statistical measurement in itself is of little value without interpretation, not just of the nature of the data and the appropriateness of a given analysis, but especially of final results. Statistical significance can sometimes be spurious; thus analysis must be reunited with theory at some point, and the research process travels full circle.

Interpretation

In the framework of strict scientific method, according to which a researcher has proposed one or more hypotheses deduced from theory and then gathered data to reject, support, or fail to reject them, interpretation would seem to be a straightforward process. The hypothesis is either rejected or not; it is either consistent with a theory or not. Of course, as we have seen, such decisions are not straightforward at all, and are even less so where a study has not been guided by such a strict deductive approach, especially where a specific theoretical model does not exist. Consider, for example, the interpretation of statistically significant correlations between two variables, a and b. Would this indicate a direct causal relationship, or are a and b both caused by some other variable, c (Wells 1985: 372)? In the absence of a sound theoretical model, it is not possible to answer this question.

Conclusions must not necessarily be proven, but rather assessed; the assessment itself can then be judged against various models. In this way, one avoids the problem of circularity – that data are always interpreted according to the very theory one is trying to prove – since assessments themselves (such as 'does comprehension precede production?', 'does there appear to be a relationship between input and acquisition?') are actually theoretically neutral (Kaplan 1984: 31). One can find assessments consistent with a number of possible theories. A well-developed field, in particular, will have both macro-theories, such as general relativity in physics and cognitivist theory in CLR, and also micro-theories (red shift; lexical development). Many competing micro-theories may all be consistent with a macro-theory. Interpretation usually functions at the level of micro-theory, or prediction, and is dependent upon both methodology and what Kaplan has called the theoretical 'neighborhoods' employed in the analysis (1984: 39). Almost all theories, at either level, will be falsified by some evidence, but unless the evidence is against the very core of the theory, it is usual to consider the data to be in error (Kaplan 1984: 107). In this manner theory does affect assessment of the data, and one must therefore consider the consequences for a discipline which has no well-developed theoretical basis.

Turning to CLR in particular, and picking up earlier themes, we note the existence of several competing 'macro-frameworks', e.g., language acquisition is a sub-type of cognitive development. Each of these frameworks, even before being judged against or used as a filter for data, must meet certain requirements, some of which are specific to given types of frameworks, others of which are generalizable to all.

For example, any theory of language acquisition must meet, according to Atkinson, the six conditions of

1 *learnability*, explaining the fact of development;
2 *equipotentiality*, i.e., of any native language to be learned with equal competency;
3 *time*, making acquisition possible within the time scale in which it occurs;
4 *input*, allowing language development to occur given empirically valid assumptions about the nature of input.;
5 *cognitivity*, consistency with what is known about children's general cognitive abilities,
6 *development*, consistency with what is understood about development in general

(1982: 220–1, referring to Pinker 1979).

If language development is to be considered not autonomous but rather explainable on the basis of some other type of development, the macro-theory will be what Atkinson has called a reducing theory, and this means that, in the case of a cognitive reducing theory, both the theoretical terms and the formal operations of the linguistic theory must be translated into and identifiable in the theory of cognition (1982: 175), as discussed in chapter 2. This also implies that language and cognition are sufficiently distinguishable, so that it can be clearly determined whether or not one will reduce to the other (Atkinson 1982: 171). Social theories, similarly, require translation of terms and identifiability of operations, but Atkinson has noted how social theorists differ from autonomists or cognitivists in not viewing the child as a 'model-builder' or 'theory-constructor' (1982: 206). Compare Chomsky's child capable of learning a language and the way that he or she is a 'little linguist', and a superior one at that (1965: 30–1).

Numerous micro-theories make up the practice of CLR which may be compatible with one, several, or even all the macro-frameworks. Bloom, for example, has been at work on the micro-theoretical issue of the relationship between Piaget's stages of cognitive operations and lexical development, issues of conceptualization and measurement which ultimately will feed into the macro-theoretical cognitivist view. Bloom, Lifter, and Broughton (1985) noted the many studies which have been interpreted as supporting one version or another of the cognitivist theory are based on the idea that language and cognition develop either serially or in parallel. These interpretations were themselves rooted in two assumptions: that tests or correspondences between the two domains necessarily suggest a relationship, and that ordinal scales of sensori-motor development, derived from Piaget's work, are an appropriate instrument for measuring the child's developing knowledge. The method-ological procedures resulting from these assumptions, however, have restricted the types of interpretations of micro-theories which researchers make, such as the assessment of the prediction that the child's first words are somehow in correspondence with his or her level of sensori-motor development. Thus, for example, it has not been possible to explore the alternative view that language and early cognition are interdependent and mutually transforming.

Although description itself entails interpretation, sometimes the intention is to go beyond description in order to make developmental or other claims in support of a theory or framework. In this case, the central problem of assessing the apparent results consists of multiple obstacles. First one must assess the degree of confidence one has in the results and whether, should there be no consensus among related studies, this means that the analysis is incorrect, or simply that children are different (Bloom et al. 1981: 407). Second, one must grapple with the problem of direct and abstract (or what Kaplan called first- and second-order) discourse. Although data themselves are primarily direct and dependent upon location, participants, systems, and other contextualizing elements, interpretations must achieve the level of second-order, abstracted discourse from which conclusions may be drawn which are invariant, neutral, and, one hopes, objective (Kaplan 1984: 34–5). It is these conclusions which tend to be featured in published work, by and large, and not the process of observation itself, with all its inherent difficulties (Fassnacht 1982: 187), from which the interpretation stems.

The first difficulty one has in determining whether one's results are essentially consistent, despite studies which may draw different conclusions, is a matter of having taken all the necessary steps methodologically to ensure that intuitions, descriptions, categorizations, and judgments are well sup-ported. It requires that data be recorded in such a way as to depict reality, meaning that neither the form in which reality is represented, nor the context, is changed in the course of an observation (Fassnacht 1982: 16). Specifically, one can accomplish this by having

1 as many data as possible which have been subject to control of setting and other aspects of collection;
2 as many subjects as feasible, or alternatively as many instances of the features in question as possible;
3 a combination of recording techniques which complement each other such that where one is defective the other is superior (e.g., videotape is non-selective; human note-taking observers are highly selective);
4 multiple observers and/or analyzers to maximize attempts at objectivity;
5 clearly and formally articulated procedures for recording;
6 consistent, well-defined coding categories;
7 reliability measures;
8 an open mind.

In short, well-designed and executed research will help to ensure confidence in one's data.

The second problem, of converting direct data into second-order discourse, cannot be accomplished by any single practitioner alone. A truly general level of interpretation is best achieved by large numbers of similar studies, with high replicability of methods (especially literal and constructive replication), so that thorough examination and re-examination of data from numerous but related studies (i.e., studies focusing on the same or related micro-theory) will gradually force interpretation into the second-order level. If researchers keep track, as they generally do, of both general and individual results, the issue of whether variation in results is due to analysis itself, or to differences among subjects, should eventually be clarified, especially where ample background information about all subjects has been provided.

Only when CLR has begun to make progress in assessing its micro-theories will it be possible to move to yet a third level of discourse – the production of an adequate, detailed, encompassing macro-theory compatible with micro-theoretical claims. Any field, CLR included, is and should be a cooperative venture. Practitioners in competition with one another tend to hinder progress in the field, as competition in interpretation frequently produces dichotomous thinking where synthesis is more beneficial. Unfortunately, the socio-political and economic structure of disciplines sometimes encourages competition, as in the quest for funding and the pursuit of strategic certainty and dependence. As Kaplan has written, most of our knowledge is of a relatively weak (i.e., indeterminate, indirect) order, leading one to the place where it is possible to 'entertain different theories, even about the same thing, that do not completely mesh', or even entertain 'theories ... in conflict' (1984: 39). The strictly dichotomous thinker, a breed which is encouraged by too-rigid adherence to the deductive model, will have difficulty rising above surface conflicts to achieve the level of macro-theory which may resolve apparently contradictory predictions. One need only consider the well-known example from physics and its reconciliation of the apparently opposing views of the nature of light. The limits of deductivism as the only acceptable form of 'proof' have also been challenged in mathematics, especially by computers capable of re-demonstrating the value of other forms of reasoning such as pictorial modes. After all, wrote one mathematician, what is a proof other than simply 'an argument that succeeds in convincing one's peers. . . . In this sense, the less formal arguments, invoking diagrams and appealing directly to intuition, are sometimes the most successful proofs' (Rival 1987: 44).

The other danger is the breed of researcher who dismisses either the level of theory or that of practice altogether, as if it were actually possible to do so. This is also a hindrance. For while to ease discussion it is common to divide a field into theory and practice, in reality an almost indissoluable link exists between the two, creating an interdependence which practitioners perhaps wish were not there. Fassnacht observed that methodological developments are sometimes 'devalued as mere servants', not attractring the esteem which accompanies theoretical developments. This attitude he found 'not only damaging, but arrogant' (Fassnacht 1982: v). Both poles are equally critical to the progress a field makes, and both are the necessary business of CLR as a whole and of any individual researcher. Were it not so, we would live in the hopeless world described by Deutsch, in which some researchers entrench themselves in the rather (they suppose) atheoretical 'analysis of countless transcripts', alongside those who 'concentrate exclusively on theorizing without taking any notice of empirical work' (1983: 143). The one population will produce reams of data with no meaning, the other, elegantly construed explanations which lack all plausibility. Indeed, some believe that this has already begun to happen in general linguistics, where the 'neo-empiricists' (such as discourse analysts) are seen as the enemy of formal theorists of grammar (Frawley 1987: 361–2), and the latter accuse the former of being utterly incapable of distinguishing the trivial from the non-trivial.

7 The Practice of the Field of CLR

Preliminary issues

When all is said and done, a discipline must be assessed according to actual practices rather than its rhetoric about them. In examining CLR, one will immediately perceive that the field does not represent any unitary approach to practice, or even a limited number of approaches. Certainly one source of this diversity is the multi-faceted nature of language itself and, consequently, the various disciplinary backgrounds of the researchers, who represent training in humanities, social sciences, and, a few, sciences. Specifically, authors of published research have been affiliated with psychology, linguistics, anthropology, medicine, philosophy, foreign languages, education, and communication disorders, among others (Bennett-Kastor 1986a). Each of these disciplines has left a mark on practice.

Concerning the value of this variety, one might assume either that theoretical and methodological disunity will hinder development in the field, or alternatively that it will create the appropriate tensions from which advanced understanding arises. Certainly it could be effectively argued that multiple approaches are a necessry condition for acquiring knowledge about a phenomenon (language) which itself is manifested in a variety of ways: physically, culturally, socially, cognitively. No one would argue seriously for a methodology which ignored crucial differences in the levels and functions of language and its use.

There are types of disunity, however, that have very little to do with the nature of the observed phenomenon. For example, consider two researchers who independently pursue the topic of the acquisition of negation in English. One researcher, A, might utilize 60 subjects balanced for gender in three groups of two-, three-, and four-year-olds, with 20 in each group. Another researcher, B, may use three children, one of whom is her own, the other two the children of colleagues or university students. Clearly, the methodological differences thus far between the two studies have nothing to do with negation itself, and yet it is quite likely that the two researchers will come to different conclusions. One may claim that B's study is better designed to examine individual differences while A's seeks a more general level, and yet a study using large numbers of subjects will not preclude an examination of individual differences since data are collected from each subject independently. Thus, *A*'s study is potentially much more informative, about both individual and general processes in acquisition.

Among the numerous approaches to assessing research practices which one might take is the strategy of examining the field diachronically. This approach will be reported here. The assessment is based on a sample of 185 published research studies which appeared in print between 1970 and 1987. At least ten studies from each year were selected from the following journals: *Journal of Child Language, First Language, Journal of Psycholinguistic Research, Language, International Journal of Psycholinguistics* which later merged with *Linguistics, Child Development, The Merrill-Palmer Quarterly, Journal of Speech and Hearing Research, Papers and Reports in Child Language Development,* and, prior to its name change, *Journal of Verbal Learning and Verbal Behavior.* These journals are associated with several disciplines. After 1974, the majority of studies were selected from *Journal of Child Language;* their authors represented no less disciplinary variety, however. Studies were selected in random manner, although studies of entirely pre-linguistic infants, and studies of language-disordered populations exclusively, were not included.

That so many journals contain articles relevant to the field is itself revealing. One might consider that having only one or two journals in the field would be advantageous, and yet if this were the case, the time lag between submission and publication might become unacceptably long, or we would require an edition every week, as is the case with *Science.* Competition between two journals might be problematic and encourage dichotomous research. Conservatism is also a danger where there are few outlets. On the other hand, the diversity of journals, while assuring that CLR has greater access to print, means that disciplinary unity is even more unlikely to arise, and also that one must do considerable searching to put together a comprehensive review of the literature for any given topic, encountering numerous unfamiliar practices and, at times, contradictory results from incompatible studies.

Studies were examined for nineteen variables. These were:

1 year of publication, grouped into three-year intervals;
2 disciplinary affiliation of the major author (where this could be ascertained);
3 topic of research (e.g. phonology-phonetics, lexical semantics, discourse);
4 data-collection setting (experimental, naturalistic, combined);
5 research design (longitudinal, cross-sectional, etc.);
6 form of language (comprehension or response, production, combined);
7 number of subjects;
8 age of subjects;
9 gender distribution among subjects;
10 method of recording;

11 reporting of the use of transcription procedures;
12 measurement instrument for the classification of subjects;
13 determination of coding categories (*a priori, post priori*, both, unclear);
14 frequency of observation sessions;
15 duration of observation sessions;
16 use of inter-observer reliability measures;
17 use of statistical measures (descriptive, non-parametric, parametric types);
18 the length of the published paper;
19 the use of illustrative materials such as tables and graphs.

Previously it was reported that several significant differences appeared when the contributions of psychologists and linguists were compared according to these variables (Bennett-Kastor 1986a). The data-base since that report appeared has been increased to include research published in 1986 and 1987, and we are asking of the data what they reveal about the development of practices in the field between 1970 and 1987. Such an exploration will provide both a profile of the field in its current state, and a topography, so to speak, of trends, forces, and other tendencies over the course of 17 years, during which time several different frameworks have passed in and out of dominance. Appendix 1 contains tables of raw data on which the following discussion is based, including calculations of approximate X^2 for each variable. These must not be taken too seriously since most of the categories are somewhat arbitrarily delimited, and expected frequences are estimated on the assumption that all possible variables are equally likely. However, it is in fact difficult to say what the expected frequencies ought to be.

In general, one might say that the earliest analyses in CLR were made at more general levels. In reading the discussion sections of papers, for example, one might encounter claims about the relationship between comprehension and production at a rather gross level. Close attention to the myriad epistemological and methodological problems involved in the act of garnering evidence for such claims came slowly to the field, and one senses both that scholars have become increasingly self-critical over the years, and that analyses of smaller and smaller aspects of language are being undertaken. This may be seen as a sign that more descriptive work has been accomplished and opened the way for increasingly detailed and ultimately more comprehensive studies.

CLR in the early seventies

Table A1.1 (Appendix 1) shows that, in the early seventies, the majority of researchers in CLR were affiliated with psychology units. One might expect that, therefore, CLR would be a primarily experimental field, and a glance at table A1.3 reveals that this is indeed the case. Exploration focused on what might be called 'micro-syntactic' issues such as negation, the development of interrogatives, and mastery of prepositions, and so on, although the period between 1973 and 1975 revealed greater interest in semantics, as manifested either in lexical morphology or syntactic constructions (active-passive, for instance).

Longitudinal studies were still not commonly undertaken, nor could it be assumed that production was the main focus. These are a consequence of the experimental method, as will be seen below. Moderate to large numbers of subjects were frequently utilized, and there was a preference for those children who were old enough to know a great deal about language already. Gender of subjects was not typically considered important enough to mention, although where it was reported, most researchers attempted to balance males and females in the earliest years. In the period between 1973 and 1975, however, male subjects were more common.

This was the era during which transformational-generativism dominated the theoretical background of research. A concern with tapping linguistic competence led to the focus on experimental studies of comprehension in older subjects. The consequences for recording data were that, often, a subject's responses were directly recorded onto some sort of stimulus material, or else audiotaped (with or without note taking as a supplement). Many authors did not report how the data were recorded, however. Researchers were as likely as not to transcribe data; table A1.15 reveals that there was little concern with reliability of either transcription or coding categorization, which tended to make use of *a priori* categories (table A1.12).

CLR could only loosely be defined as a developmentally oriented field, since the categorization of subjects on the basis of age was not routinely undertaken. In fact, throughout the history of the discipline, it has tended to be the case that subjects are categorized in no single manner. Where one researcher uses age or MLU, several others will use the child's reponse to a stimulus, or the type of stimulus the child receives, or some other basis for classification. It is in fact interesting to see that MLU has not been relied upon at all well as a sole measure of the language by which a child is categorized.

Small frequencies in the cells of the tables on observation sessions (tables A1.13 and A1.14) are symptomatic of the reliance at this time on experimental research which did not involve multiple contacts with the subjects, but only single sessions of relatively (usually) short duration. Concerning analysis of data, the tendency in 1970–2 for two or more types of statistical analyses to be undertaken is consistent with the use of relatively large numbers of subjects in highly controlled settings. Towards the mid-seventies one observes an increase in the number of studies relying solely on descriptive statistics (or none at all); this parallels an increase in less-controlled, naturalistic settings (pp. 107, 119).

Two variables concern the communication of results: length of published paper, and use of illustrative material. The length of a paper may be related both to the degree to which data are summarized quantitatively and the use of technical vocabulary which is operationalized for the field as a whole and need not be explicated with long, descriptive passages. It also reflects editorial policy to a certain extent – *Journal of Child Language*, for example, has a rather strict twenty-page limit (though this is occasionally violated); articles in *Language*, of which few concern CLR, are often considerably long; papers in journals under the jurisdiction of the American Psychological Association, or those which recommend APA guidelines in the preparation of manuscripts (*Child Development*, for instance, or *Journal of Verbal Learning and Verbal Behavior*), are apt to be short. Format is formulaic.

At first, one may question whether the use of illustrative material is especially important. Its importance has not in fact made much of an impact on the field, although, as Cleveland has observed, there has been a graphics revolution in a number of fields, especially statistical science (1985: 18). Graphs are powerful tools both for analysis of data, and for their presentation. Computer graphics have contributed considerably to the graphics movement; table A1.18 shows that, in the early seventies, graphic presentation of results was not especially important. Tabular presentation was, however, commonly used, and its use has been consistent. Woods, Fletcher, and Hughes summarized the primary purpose of illustrative material as the communication of the data more readily 'without distorting its [sic] general import' (1986: 21). The publication manual of the American Psychological Association cautioned that figures and tables should supplement, but not replace, the text itself. Thus, they should be used sparingly; especially figures, which are expensive to reproduce, should be used only where tabular form is inadequate to show trends and interactions (American Psychological Association 1974: 18).

One might summarize the period of research in CLR between 1970 and 1975 as one in which CLR was fundamentally a sub-discipline of psychology. Its research results were presented for the most part in terse, well-quantified, and tabulated form, as were most research reports in the social sciences.

CLR in the mid to late seventies

This period in CLR, which spans the turn of the decade, is represented by something of an upheaval in the trends of the earlier period. In 1976–8 slightly more linguists than psychologists contributed research, and there was an increase in contributions from scholars associated with the humanities in general as well. Although by 1981 psychologists came to dominate again, the field was nevertheless altered in distinct ways. The dominant topic of focus was no longer narrowly grammatical, but instead concerned lexical semantics, functional–pragmatic perspectives on meaning, syntax-semantics, and phonology. With the exception of the latter concern, one might characterize this period as essentially semantic. Naturalistic methods of data collection, as indicated in table A1.3, and longitudinal studies became predominant, replacing the fundamentally experimental approaches of the early seventies. Theoretically, this was an era of functional approaches as well; the limits of generative grammar as an appropriate framework for CLR had been reached, and the field was seemingly permanently altered to examine production of language rather than comprehension or grammaticality judgments (table A1.5).

A shift in the numbers of subjects utilized accompanied the other changes in methodology and perspective. Small-to-moderate numbers of subjects became common, and there was increased interest, especially in the period between 1976 and 1978, in children just on the threshold of linguistic expression (table A1.7). It was still common not to specify gender, although there was a slight preference exhibited for girls.

Also in this period we note an increased use of both supplemented audiotape and of videotape. Stimulus materials which themselves form a record were not typical. Alarmingly, there was a strong trend to fail to report the recording method. Nevertheless, transcription certainly became the norm, so data were being filtered through an additional process more often than not.

In 1976–8, more experimentation in the methods of measuring subjects occurred, especially through the use of combined techniques, but age was settled upon as the most appropriate measure in the early 1980s. *A priori* categories for coding data remained the norm, although it was more often unclear just what the source of these categories might have been.

With the rise of naturalistic, longitudinally based research, the questions of frequency and duration of observation sessions became significant. Few researchers appreciated the possibilities of very frequent observation – most found that recordings made once a week at the most, and more typically once every ten days or so, seemed to suffice. Duration was probably inadequate, usually half an hour or less, although by the 1980s more studies began incorporating long observation sessions of 60 or even 90 minutes.

Reliability measures had not yet become routine in CLR; if anything, in fact, quantitative information was less routinely utilized during this period. In 1976–8, out of 31 studies, 21 utilized only descriptive statistics; in 1979–81, of 33 studies, more of a balance occurs in the use of descriptive and inferential measures (table A1.16. Again, one assumes a relationship between naturalistic studies with small N and the lack of statistical treatment.

During this period, especially 1979–81, papers grew in length. This again suggests a link between quantification and economy of expression. The nature of the coding, which during this period was often semantic and/or functional, also may have contributed to length since a great deal of controversy surrounded selection of categories and their justification. The period between 1979 and 1981 exhibited increased use of both tables and figures; one also may note the use of correlation statistics during this period. Since graphical methods often better depict correlations, this may be an explanation for the parallel increases in length, correlation measures, and illustrative material.

Recent practice of the field

The last five years in CLR publications evidence a field that is achieving some balance in terms of the disciplinary affiliations of its practitioners. Those associated with social sciences in the broad sense have come to be the major contributors, as in the early years, and yet the practices which in the past emerged with a rise in the contributions of linguists have been retained, so that the field is no longer adequately characterized as fundamentally experimental (tables A1.3 and A1.4). Semantics (lexical and sentence), discourse, and, to an extent, phonology have been the dominant topics; the last is associated especially with a hearty proportion of researchers coming from the field of communicative disorders. Although semantics remains popular, functional approaches have largely been replaced by, on the one hand, studies of lexical development and, on the other hand, examinations of language in its discourse or conversational context.

Longitudinal and cross-sectional designs have become the preferred form of research, using either very small or moderate numbers of subjects (table A1.6). Large N is uncommon, as are studies of older (school-age) children. The preference for language production has been retained from the mid-seventies. Researchers have been more careful about reporting gender distribution than they have about ensuring that males and females are equally represented.

The last years, especially, have shown an increased reliance on videotaped methods of recording. It is quite likely that this trend is related to utilization of subjects under the age of three. This has also been accompanied by a clear tendency to transcribe the record, and to report that such transcription was undertaken.

Concerning issues of analysis, the most recently published authors have made an apparently strong commitment to coding categories selected prior to data collection. By the same token, although chronological categorization of subjects was the mode in 1982–4, this did not continue into the middle 1980s. In fact, despite the large numbers of longitudinal or cross-sectional studies, only one published paper reported the use of age alone as a form of measurement. Most studies still rely on measures of a variety of sorts, or a combination of age and other measures. The field could not on the whole be considered developmental, although it appeared to be so in the early part of this decade.

Frequency of data collection, while less often reported as 'irregular', has not significantly increased during the latest years of research. Intervals of greater than two weeks are favored to a small degree, and yet duration has somewhat increased. It is interesting that more authors perceived the importance of reporting frequency than duration, which centered upon 31–60 minute periods (table A1.13 and A1.14).

As *a priori* coding categories are again favored, so is a welcome change in the practice of reliability analyses. As of 1985–7, it is almost as common as not to attempt some control over judgments of the accuracy of categorization and/or transcription. A shift back toward statistical measurement has occurred as well, despite the use of somewhat fewer numbers of subjects. It is intriguing to note, in this regard, that the number of studies undertaken by linguists and those associated with the humanities (N = 7) is nearly the same as the number of studies utilizing descriptive statistics only – or none at all (N = 8).

One would on the basis of this expect that papers would be somewhat shorter than during the era when inferential measures were less often undertaken, and this is by and large the case. Papers may still be moderately long, but very few exceed 20 pages. The use of illustrative materials has not changed significantly. Tabular presentation remains the norm; less often one encounters both tables and figures; but the so-called 'graphics revolution' of which Cleveland (1985) wrote has not evidently made its way into the field.

In summary, one can discern three rather distinct periods in the short history of CLR. First, we see a field that is quite clearly a branch of psychology, and specifically of experimental psychology. It was a field concerned with tapping a subject's comprehension of language which favored older subjects in rather large numbers so that data, which did not necessarily require transcription, might be fitted into predetermined categories and evaluated quantitatively, then presented in condensed, non-discursive articles which made rather heavy use of tables.

The second period, covering the middle seventies to the turn of the decade, is characterized by an influx of practitioners from linguistics who did not necessarily subscribe to the experimentally based, causally oriented research goals of psychologists. At first, this meant that data were collected in naturalistic settings with longitudinal designs, and analyses heavily favored language production. Smaller numbers of somewhat younger subjects could now be used, since interest was not primarily in tapping comprehension or eliciting grammaticality judgments. More use was being made of recording methods which captured the context of utterances and not just the utterances themselves, and, for the most part, inferential measures were not viewed as especially important. More graphics were utilized, and at the same time papers grew more discursive.

Finally, in the current era, the practice of CLR is still considerably eclectic, but without the obvious disciplinary alliances of the earlier years. Linguists and psychologists both might use either experimental or naturalistic settings, and the field is no longer strongly experimental nor naturalistic, design no longer predominately of one type or another. More researchers have returned to examinations of perception or comprehension, and one senses a compromise has occurred in the issue of how many subjects to use, as well as their gender distribution. Pre-schoolers are still somewhat favored. More extensive filtering of data through taping and transcription is reported, reliability has increased, and in many other respects it would appear that scholars from diverse disciplines have learned from one another's practices. Disciplinary chauvinism is by no means evident. One can safely say that the field has evolved and become truly inter-disciplinary, although much progress might still be made in the rigorousness of methodological decisions such as frequency and duration of observation, categorization of subjects, increased reliability measures, and graphical analyses of data.

Praxical clusters

We have emphasized in various places the interdependence not just of theory and method but of aspects of methodology. Although one can examine variables such as number of subjects and method of recordings as if they were distinct, methodology is in fact systematic, and certain practices turn out to be more strongly associated with other practices than one might think. Of such interdependence, one can recognize three types. The first type might be called logistic (practical) interdependence. In this category would be included the strong associations between design and numbers of subjects, for example. Longitudinal research designs are overwhelmingly associated with small numbers, not because they necessarily entail this, but because of the enormous logistical problems involved in making longitudinal records. Similarly, cross-sectional designs are associated more often with large N. One can calculate, in fact, the degree of redundancy, or alternatively informativity, of a particular research practice, using a formula derived from information theory. Attneave provides the following formula for estimating the zero-order of H, where H is a measure of redundancy, as

$$H_O = \Sigma p \log\frac{1}{p} = m \left(\frac{1}{m} \log m\right) = \log m$$

assuming that zero is the highest order of redundancy (1959: 20). By this measure, where row (R) refers to research design and column (C) to number of subjects, the measure H (R:C) = 1.1948, i.e., the information in the row given the column is fairly low. A chi-square calculated for the differences among designs in numbers of subjects is significant: X^2 (24) = 128.74, p. $\leq$ .001.

In other cases, interdependence might be called 'praxical', i.e., the result of a reasoned association between or among items which cluster together. For example, the clustering of setting and statistical treatment is of this nature, since naturalistic data are, some have argued (see chapter 6), ill suited to the assumptions of parametric measures. Where R = setting and C = statistical measurement, H (R:C) = 1.2501; X^2 (18) = 50.50, p. $\leq$ .001.

In yet other cases, one might call the interdependence simply incidental, or even spurious. For example, there is a moderate association between gender distribution of subjects and the use of illustrative material, H (R:C) = 1.8269; X^2 (12) = 32.64, p. $\leq$ .01, but this is clearly spurious. On the other hand, the association between age of subjects and frequency of observation seems to be merely incidental, a result of the fact that the youngest subjects are rarely involved in experimental designs, for which frequency is not applicable: H (R:C) = 1.5075; X^2 (24) = 116.39, p. $\leq$ .001. These examples are clear illustrations of the principle that statistical significance in itself does not ensure reliability; and there are several clusters of associations that might fall into any of the three categories.

Appendix 2 contains significant and probably not spurious associations of research practices. One would assume that the measure of a discipline's maturity can be gauged in large part by its methods and, especially the praxical clusterings of these. That it is at times difficult to assess the nature of associations among CLR methods suggests that the field has not been in existence as a distinct enterprise long enough for it to have achieved maturity. The recent methodological history of the field, as of other fields, is marked by trends which are not always especially long-lived.

A number of factors contribute to the methodological or praxical profile of CLR. Among these is the failure of many graduate departments, especially in linguistics, to offer explicit training in research design, but rather to rely upon the student's abilities to acquire methodology simply by exposure to published research. Obviously, this will tend merely to perpetuate the configuration of diverse methods which has appeared historically, causing incidental inter-dependence to be retained. Related to this is the fact that there are few centers of CLR training where an apprenticeship system might be established.

Another factor is research which focuses on a specific topic for a brief period of time. Data may be collected too narrowly; each study requires the re-establishment of the subject pool, analytical procedures, and record-keeping processes. The lack of longevity also inhibits longitudinal designs and precludes apprenticeships. Quick, 'in-and-out' style research might be the result of the so-called 'publish-or-perish' system in the universities which encourages younger scholars to produce quantities of research and makes it difficult for them to afford the luxury of sustained data collection over the course of several years. It may also favor single, independent researchers where the members of tenure and promotion committees come from disciplines unfamiliar with the concept of joint authorship. For example, it is rare in the humanities for scholars to participate in joint research efforts.

Some have claimed that economic and political factors in the awarding of federal grants discourage innovation in research techniques. Certainly one could argue that a 'rich get richer' system exists, and, given that this may be the case, a researcher may be reluctant to change his or her practices if the old methods have been successful in securing funding. This, however, is as likely to eliminate unnecessary diversity as to cause it.

Ultimately, the field of CLR stands out as a distinctly interdisciplinary one which consequently faces sure challenges to unity, whether on the level of theory or praxis. It is a challenge impossible to avoid, simply because of the nature of the topic, and which, when successfully met, will represent a significant rite of passage for a still-emerging discipline.

APPENDIX 1
Data for chapter 7
Methods matrices

Table A1.1 Year x disciplinary affiliation of major author

	Psychology	Linguistics	Communication disorders	Education	Social sciences	Other humanities	Other
1970–2	12	3	1	5	3	0	6
1973–5	13	4	5	1	3	1	3
1976–8	10	12	3	0	1	4	1
1979–81	14	8	1	4	1	1	4
1982–4	7	8	5	2	2	1	6
1985–7	8	4	8	4	3	3	0
total	64	39	23	16	13	10	20

approximate χ^2 (30) = 54.86, p. $\leq$ .01

Table A1.2 Year x topical focus of research

	Phonology/ phonetics	Lexical semantics/ morphology	Syntax/ grammar	Functional semantics/ pragmatics	Syntax-semantics	Discourse	Written language	Meta-language	Other
1970–2	5	4	7	2	5	2	2	0	3
1973–5	2	10	4	2	7	1	1	0	3
1976–8	6	6	2	3	6	2	1	0	5
1979–81	4	6	0	5	6	4	0	4	4
1982–4	2	9	3	2	2	7	3	1	2
1985–7	5	7	3	2	5	7	1	0	0
total	24	42	19	16	31	23	8	5	17

approximate χ^2 (40) = 58.03 p. $\leq$ .05

Table A1.3 Year x setting for data collection

	Experimentally elicited	Naturalistic	Combined
1970–2	20	5	5
1973–5	15	9	6
1976–8	12	18	1
1979–81	14	12	7
1982–4	11	17	3
1985–7	14	15	1
total	86	76	23

approximate χ^2 (10) = 28.07, p. $\leq$ .01

Table A1.4 Year x design

	Experimental design	Cross-sectional	Longitudinal	Combined designs
1970–2	17	9	3	1
1973–5	16	8	5	1
1976–8	12	3	15	1
1979–81	16	6	9	2
1982–4	11	12	8	0
1985–7	9	9	11	1
total	81	47	51	6

approximate χ^2 (15) = 24.46, p. $\leq$ .10

Table A1.5 Year x form of language

	Comprehension or response	Production	Combined forms
1970–2	13	12	5
1873–5	11	11	8
1976–8	5	18	8
1979–81	5	21	7
1982–4	9	18	4
1985–7	6	20	4
total	49	100	36

approximate χ^2 (10) = 15.23 p. $\leq$ .20

Table A1.6   Year x number of subjects

	1–5	6–15	16–35	36–75	over 75
1970–2	4	3	8	7	8
1973–5	5	3	8	6	8
1976–8	10	8	4	5	4
1979–81	7	7	8	7	4
1982–4	8	5	6	8	4
1985–7	9	3	11	5	2
total	43	29	45	38	30

approximate χ^2 (20) = 24.78 p. ≤ .50

Table A1.7   Year x age of subjects

	0–2	3–5	6–10	10+
1970–2	2	13	9	6
1973–5	5	8	12	5
1976–8	14	9	5	3
1979–81	8	13	8	4
1982–4	11	9	6	5
1985–7	13	9	7	1
total	53	61	47	24

approximate χ^2 (15) = 29.15, p. ≤ .02

Table A1.8   Year x gender distribution of subjects

	More male	More female	Male = female	Unspecified
1970–2	4	3	9	13
1973–5	10	4	4	12
1976–8	6	7	6	12
1979–81	7	8	6	12
1982–4	7	4	9	11
1985–7	5	11	8	6
total	39	37	42	67

approximate χ^2 (15) = 17.16, p. ≤ .50

Table A1.9 Year x method of recording data

	Audio	Video	Note/diary	Audio + Note	Video + Audio/note	Stim. Mater.	Unsp.
1970–2	7	0	3	5	1	6	8
1973–5	6	1	5	5	1	4	8
1976–8	4	3	2	9	4	2	7
1979–81	1	4	1	8	2	2	15
1982–4	5	2	3	4	5	4	8
1985–7	7	6	2	4	5	3	3
total	30	16	16	35	18	21	49

Video + audio/note – videotape supplemented with audiotape, note-taking, or both
Stim. mater. – stimulus materials on which data were directly recorded
Unsp – unspecified recording method
approximate χ^2 (30) = 74.9, p. $\leq$ .001

Table A1.10 Year x transcription practices

	Yes	No	Unclear
1970–2	11	12	7
1973–5	9	10	11
1976–8	14	4	13
1979–81	15	8	10
1982–4	14	5	12
1985–7	17	6	7
total	80	45	60

yes – author reported having transcribed the data
no – data did not require transcription
unclear – data may have required transcription, but author did
not report it.
approximate χ^2 (10) = 20.62, p. $\leq$ .05

Table A1.11 Year x measurement of subjects

	Age/grade	MLU	Other	Combined	Unclear/none/unsp.
1970–2	8	1	11	5	5
1973–5	6	1	18	3	2
1976–8	0	0	14	15	2
1979–81	11	3	8	6	5
1982–4	13	0	6	4	8
1985–7	1	2	16	10	1
total	39	7	73	43	23

approximate χ^2 (20) = p. $\leq$ .001

Table A1.12 Year x determination of coding categories

	A priori	Post priori	Unclear	Both
1970–2	19	2	6	3
1973–5	12	7	10	1
1976–8	12	3	14	2
1979–81	15	9	7	2
1982–4	13	10	4	4
1985–87	22	3	5	0
total	93	34	46	12

approximate χ^2 (15) = 34.07, p. $\leq$ .01

Table A1.13 Year x frequency of observation

	No. of observations						
	4–5 per week	2–3 per week	1 per week	1 per 2 weeks	1 per 2 weeks +	irreg.	NA[a]
1970–2	0	0	0	0	1	3	26
1973–5	1	0	3	2	0	1	23
1976–8	0	1	5	1	7	3	14
1979–81	0	1	1	3	3	1	24
1982–4	0	0	1	1	2	4	23
1985–7	0	2	1	3	5	2	17
total	1	4	11	10	18	14	127

[a] not applicable since research required a single observation only
approximate χ^2 (30) = 46.28, p. $\leq$ .05

Table A1.14 Year x duration of observation session (in minutes)

	Over 90	61–90	31–60	1–30	Unspec.	NA
1970–2	0	0	1	5	4	20
1973–5	1	2	0	3	5	19
1976–8	1	0	3	10	8	9
1979–81	3	2	2	4	5	17
1982–4	3	1	5	4	6	12
1985–7	0	1	6	5	4	14
total	8	6	17	31	32	91

approximate χ^2 (25) = 38.91, p. $\leq$ .05

Table A1.15   Year x reliability

	Yes	*No*
1970–2	5	25
1973–5	8	22
1976–8	2	29
1979–81	8	25
1982–4	8	23
1985–7	14	16
total	45	140

approximate χ^2 (5) = 15.20, p. ≤ .01

Table A1.16   Year x statistical analysis

	Non/descriptive only (frequency, etc.)	*Non-parametric tests*			*Parametric tests*			
		χ^2	r/r$_s$	Total	t	Anova	2 or more	Total
1970–2	*6*	2	1	*3*	2	6	13	*21*
1973–5	*13*	1	1	*2*	0	3	12	*15*
1976	*21*	0	1	*1*	0	2	7	*9*
1979–81	*14*	0	5	*5*	1	1	12	*14*
1982–4	*10*	2	1	*3*	1	4	13	*18*
1985–7	*8*	1	3	*4*	1	3	14	*18*
total	72	6	12	18	5	19	71	95

approximate χ^2 (10) = 74.33, p. ≤ .001 (italicized totals only)

Table A1.17   Year x length of published paper (pages)

	1–10	*11–20*	*21+*
1970–2	15	13	2
1973–5	14	15	1
1976–8	5	23	3
1979–81	2	19	12
1982–4	9	18	4
1985–7	10	17	3
total	55	105	25

approximate χ^2 (10) = 34.37, p. ≤ .001

Table A1.18   Year x illustrative material

	Tables	*Figures*	*Both*	*Neither*
1970–2	18	2	5	5
1973–5	18	4	5	3
1976–8	18	1	10	2
1979–81	16	2	12	3
1982–4	18	1	10	5
1985–7	17	2	11	0
total	105	12	15	53

approximate χ^2 (15) = 19.27, p. $\leq$ .50

APPENDIX 2
Data for chapter 7
Praxical clusters

Tables portray interdependencies between methodological variables significant at the 0.001 level for approximate chi-squares. Significant interdependencies which were clearly spurious have been eliminated, as have certain others that appeared to be incidental. The formula for and explanation of measure of H_0 is found in chapter seven.

Table A2.1 Discipline x statistical analysis

	None/descriptive	χ^2	*r*	*Anova*	*t-test*	*2 or more types*
Psychology	18	1	7	4	2	32
Linguistics	31	0	0	1	1	6
Communication						
disorders	3	0	2	9	0	9
Education	3	1	1	2	1	8
Social sciences	0	2	1	3	1	6
Other humanities	8	0	0	0	0	2
other	9	2	1	0	0	8

approximate χ^2 (36) = 98.54; H (C:R) = 1.6414

Table A2.2 Setting x statistical analysis

	None/descriptive	χ^2	*r*	*Anova*	*t-test*	*2 or more types*
Experimentally						
elicited	17	3	2	15	4	45
Naturalistic	45	3	8	2	0	18
Combined	10	0	2	1	2	8

approximate χ^2 (10) = 50.50; H (R:C) = 1.2501

Table A2.3   Design x statistical analysis

	None/descriptive	χ^2	*r*	*Anova*	*t-test*	*2 or more types*
longitudinal	35	1	4	3	0	8
cross-sectional	14	1	3	7	2	20
combined	5	0	0	0	0	1
experimental	18	4	5	9	3	42

approximate χ^2 (15) = 45.24; H (R:C) = 1.5204

Table A2.4   Topic x form of language

	Comprehension or response	*Production*	*Combined*
Phonology/phonetics	4	19	1
lexical semantics/ morphology	11	19	12
Syntax/grammar	7	10	2
Functional semantics/ pragmatics	2	11	3
Syntax-semantics	14	12	5
Discourse	2	16	5
Written language	4	3	1
Metalanguage	4	0	1
Other	1	10	6

approximate χ^2 (16) = 40.11; H (C:R) = 1.2905

Table A2.5   Topic x recording method

	Audio	*Video*	*Note/diary*	*Audio + note*	*Video + audio/note[a]*	*Stim mater.*	*Unsp.*
Phonology/phonetics	9	0	3	6	2	4	0
Lexical semantics/ morphology	3	1	6	8	3	13	8
Syntax/grammar	4	3	2	2	1	5	2
Functional semantics/ pragmatics	2	4	0	1	4	5	0
Syntax-semantics	3	1	4	12	3	7	1
Discourse	3	6	0	2	5	7	0
Written language	1	0	0	0	0	0	7
Metalanguage	1	0	0	0	0	4	0
other	4	1	1	4	0	4	3

Video + audio/note – videotape supplemented with audiotape, note-taking, or both
Stim. mater – stimulus materials on which data were directly recorded
Unsp – unspecified recording method
[a] Categories collapsed after calculation of chi-square

approximate χ^2 (64) = 122.16; H (C:R) = 2.3476

Table A2.6   Data setting x transcription practices

	Yes + detail provided[a]	Yes, no detail	No	Unclear
Experimentally elicited	10	9	32	35
Naturalistic	33	16	8	19
Combined	7	5	5	6

[a] record was transcribed, and the author provided details concerning the form of the transcription.

approximate χ^2 (6) = 38.37; H (R:C) = 1.2974

Table A2.7   Design x transcription

	Yes + detail provided	Yes, no detail	No	Unclear
Longitudinal	22	9	6	14
Cross-sectional	14	9	10	14
Combined	0	4	0	2
Experimental	14	8	29	30

approximate χ^2 (9) = 30.72; H (R:C) = 1.5770

Table A2.8   Data x recording method

	Audio	Video	Note/diary	Audio + note	Video + audio/note[a]	Stim. mater.	Unsp.
Experimentally elicited	16	3	5	10	2	31	19
Naturalistic	9	12	9	21	15	8	2
Combined	5	1	2	4	1	10	0

Video + audio/note – videotape supplemented with audiotape, note-taking, or both
Stim. mater. – stimulus materials on which data were directly recorded
Unsp. – unspecified recording method
[a] Categories collapsed after calculation of chi-square

approximate χ^2 (16) = 69.17; H (R:C) = 1.1773

Table A2.9   Data x number of subjects

	1–5	*6–15*	*16–35*[a]	*36–75*[a]	*over 75*
Experimentally elicited	2	10	25	24	25
Naturalistic	37	17	14	7	1
Combined	4	2	6	7	4

[a] Categories collapsed after calculation of chi-square
approximate χ^2 (16) = 94.00; H (R:C) = 1.0805

Table A2.10   Data setting x age of subjects

	0–2	*3–5*	*6–10*	*over 10*
Experimentally elicited	7	30	36	13
Naturalistic	40	25	5	6
Combined	6	6	6	5

approximate χ^2 (6) = 62.03; H (R:C) = 1.2051

Table A2.11   Data x form of language

	Comprehension or response	*Production*	*Combined*
Experimentally elicited	45	18	23
Naturalistic	2	67	7
Combined	2	15	6

approximate χ^2 (4) = 93.16; H (R:C) = 1.0838

Table A2.12   Design of study x number of subjects

	1–5	*6–15*	*16–35*[a]	*36–75*[a]	*over 75*
Longitudinal	34	13	3	1	0
Cross-sectional	2	3	14	13	15
Combined	2	0	1	3	0
Experimental	5	13	27	21	13

[a] Categories collapsed after calculation of chi-square
approximate χ^2 (24) = 128.74; H (R:C) = 1.1948

Table A2.13 Design x age of subjects

	0–2	*3–5*	*6–10*	*over 10*
Longitudinal	38	9	3	1
Cross-sectional	3	21	12	11
Combined	2	3	1	0
Experimental	10	28	31	12

approximate χ^2 (9) = 90.66; H (R:C) = 1.3433

Table A2.14 Design x form of language

	Comprehension or response	*Production*	*Combined*
Longitudinal	2	43	6
Cross-sectional	14	25	8
Combined	1	5	0
Experimental	32	27	22

approximate χ^2 (6) = 42.45; H (C:R) = 1.2814

Table A2.15 Form of language x number of subjects

	1–5	*6–15*	*16–35*[a]	*36–75*[a]	*over 75*
Comprehension or response	1	3	15	17	13
Production	39	20	21	8	12
Combined	3	6	9	13	5

[a] Categories collapsed after calculation of chi-square
approximate χ^2 (16) = 65.04; H (R:C) = 1.1933

Table A2.16 Form of language x age of subjects

	0–2	*3–5*	*6–10*	*over 10*
Comprehension or response	5	18	21	5
Production	42	36	11	11
Combined	6	7	15	8

approximate χ^2 (6) = 40.71; H (R:C) = 1.2882

Table A2.17   Number of subjects x age of subjects

	0–2	*3–5*	*6–10*	*over 10*
1–5	31	10	1	1
6–15	13	11	4	1
16–35[a]	6	24	13	2
36–75[a]	3	10	18	7
over 75	0	6	11	13

[a] Categories collapsed after calculation of chi-square
approximate χ^2 (24) = 128.43; H (C:R) = 1.4606

Table A2.18   Form of language x reliability

	Yes	*No*
Comprehension or response	3	46
Production	34	66
Combined	8	28

approximate χ^2 (2) = 16.35; H (C:R) = 0.7366

Table A2.19   Form of language x length of published report

	1–10 pp.	*11–20 pp.*	*over 20 pp.*
Comprehension or response	24	24	1
Production	20	61	19
Combined	11	20	5

approximate χ^2 (4) = 19.02; H (C:R) = 1.3001

Table A2.20 Recording method x transcription practices

	Yes + detail provided	Yes, no detail	No	Unclear
Audio	9	11	3	7
Video	9	3	1	3
Note/diary	0	3	10	3
Audio + note	15	9	1	10
Video + audio/note[a]	12	3	0	3
Stim. mater.	4	1	10	34
Unsp.	1	0	20	0

Video + audio/note – videotape supplemented with audiotape, note-taking, or both
Stim. mater. – stimulus materials on which data were directly recorded
Unsp. – unspecified recording method
[a] Categories collapsed after calculation of chi-squares

approximate χ^2 (24) = 156.07; H (C:R) = 1.3502

Table A2.21 Transcription practices x reliability

	yes	no
yes, detail provided	22	28
yes, no detail	9	21
no transcription	9	36
unclear	5	55

approximate χ^2 (3) = 20.57; H (C:R) = 0.7202

References

Aaronson, D. and Rieber, R. (eds) 1979. Psycholinguistic research: Duplications and applications. Hillsdale, NJ: Lawrence Erlbaum Associates.

Achenbach, T. 1978. *Research in Developmental Psychology: Concepts, strategies, methods.* New York: Free Press.

Ackerman, B. 1983. Children's judgments of the functional acceptability of referential communication in discourse contexts. *JCL* 10, 151–66.

Aitchison, J. 1983. *The Articulate Mammal: An introduction to psycholinguistics,* 2nd edn. London: Hutchinson.

American Psychological Association. 1974. *Publication Manual,* 2nd edn. Washington, DC: American Psychological Association.

Amidan, A. and Carey, P. 1972. Why five-year-olds cannot understand before and after. *Journal of Verbal Learning and Verbal Behavior* 11, 417–23.

Anderson, B. 1971. *The Psychology Experiment,* 2nd edn. Belmont: Wadsworth.

Andrick, G. and Tager-Flusberg, H. 1986. The acquisition of colour terms. *JCL* 13, 119–34.

Anselmi, D., Tomasello, M. and Acunzo, M. 1986. Young children's responses to neutral and specific contingent queries. *JCL* 13, 135–44.

Antinucci, F. and Miller, R. 1976. How children talk about what happened. *JCL* 3, 167–89.

Arlman-Rupp, A., van Niekirk de Haan, D. and van de Sandt-Koenderman, M. 1976. Brown's early stages: some evidence from Dutch. *JCL* 3, 267–74.

Aronoff, M. 1985. Orthography and linguistic theory. *Language* 61, 28–72.

Atkinson, M. 1982. *Explanations in the Study of Child Language Development.* Cambridge: Cambridge University Press.

Attneave, F. 1959. *Applications of Information Theory to Psychology.* New York: Holt, Rinehart, Winston.

Baldie, B. 1976. The acquisition of the passive voice. *JCL* 3, 331–48.

Barnes, S., Gutfreund, M., Satterly, D. and Wells, G. 1983. Characteristics of adult speech which predict children's language development. *JCL* 10, 65–84.

Barrie-Blackley, S. 1973. Six-year-old children's understanding of setences adjoined with time adverbs. *Journal of Psycholinguistic Research* 2, 153–65.

Barton, D. 1975. Statistical significance in phonemic perception experiments. *JCL* 2, 297–8.

Bates, E., Camaioni, L., and Volterra, V. 1975. The acquisition of performatives prior to speech. *Merrill-Palmer Quarterly* 21, 205–26.

Bates, E. and MacWhinney, B. 1982. Functionalist approaches to grammar. In E.

Wanner and L. Gleitman (eds), *Language Acquisition: The state of the art*. Cambridge: Cambridge University Press.

Beaudichon, J. 1973. Nature and instrumental function of private speech in problem-solving situations. *Merrill-Palmer Quarterly* 19, 117–35.

—— 1978. Structure and efficiency in child communication. *International Journal of Psycholinguistics* 5:3, 59–73.

Beckey, R. 1942. A study of certain factors related to retardation of speech. *Journal of Speech Disorders* 7, 223–49.

Beckwith, R., Bloom, L., Albury, D., Raqib, A., and Booth, R. 1985. Technology and methodology. *Transcript Analysis* 2, 72–5.

Beckwith, R., Rispoli, M., and Bloom, L. 1984. Child language and linguistic theory: in response to Nina Hyams. *JCL* 11, 685–7.

Bellugi, U. 1965. The development of interrogative structures in children's speech. In K. Riegel (ed.), *The Development of Language Functions*, University of Michigan Language Development Program, report no. 8.

Bennett-Kastor, T. 1983. Noun phrases and coherence in child narratives. *JCL* 10, 135–49.

—— 1986a. The two fields of child language research. *First Language* 6, 161–74.

—— 1986b. Cohesion and predication in child narrative. *JCL* 13, 353–70.

—— Forthcoming. Utterance repetition and social development: A case study of Genie and her caregiver.

Bennett-(Kastor), T. and Lowell, E. 1977. A functional alternative to mean length of utterance as a tool for assessment of communicative development. 5th International Salzburg Linguistics Tagung.

Berelson, B. and Steiner, G. 1964. *Human Behavior*. New York: Harcourt, Brace and World.

Berger, M. (ed.) 1970. *Videotape Techniques in Psychiatric Training and Treatment*. New York: Bruner/Mazel.

Berko, J. 1958. The child's learning of English morphology. *Word* 14, 150–77.

Berko, J. and Brown, R. 1960. Psycholinguistic research methods. In P. Mussen (ed.), *Handbook of Research Methods in Child Development*. New York: John Wiley.

Bernstein, M. 1983. Formation of internal structure in a lexical category. *JCL* 10, 381–99.

—— 1984. Non-linguistic responses to verbal instructions. *JCL* 11, 293–311.

Berry, M. and Erickson, R. 1973. Speaking rate: Effects on children's comprehension of normal speech, *JSHR* 16, 367–74.

Bever, T., Mehler, J. and Valian, V. 1967. Linguistic capacity of very young children. Lecture, Graduate School of Education, Harvard University. Cited in D. McNeill, *The Acquisition of Language: The study of developmental psycholinguistics*, New York: Harper.

Blake, J., Austin, W. and Lowenstein, J. 1987. The effect of enactment upon sentence imitation in preschool children. *Journal of Psycholinguistic Research* 16, 351–67.

Blank, M. 1975. Eliciting verbalization from young children in experimental tasks: A methodological note. *Child Development* 46, 254–7.

Blank, M. and Frank, S. 1971. Story recall in kindergarten children: effect of method of presentation on psycholinguistic performance. *Child Development* 42, 299–312.

Blasdell, R. and Jensen, P. 1970. Stress and word position as determinants of imitation in first-language learners. *JSHR* 13, 193–202.

Bloch, O. 1921. Les premiers stades du langage de l'enfant. *Journal de Psychologie* 18, 693–712.

Block, E. and Kessel, F. 1980. Determinants of the acquisition order of grammatical morphemes: A re-analysis and re-interpretation. *JCL* 7, 181–8.

Bloom, L. 1970. *Language Development: Form and function in emerging grammars.* Cambridge, Mass.: MIT Press.

—— 1973. *One Word at a Time.* The Hague: Mouton.

—— 1974a. Talking, understanding, and thinking. In R. Schiefelbusch and L. Lloyd (eds), *Language Perspectives – Acquisition, Retardation, and Intervention*, Baltimore: University Park Press.

—— 1974b. Commentary on Schacter et al.. Monographs of the society for research in child development. Boston: Society for Research in Child Development.

—— 1983. Tensions in psycholinguistics. Review of *Language Acquisition: The state of the art* by E. Wanner and L. Gleitman (eds). *Science* 220, 843–4.

—— 1984. Review of *Explanation in the study of language development*, by M. Atkinson *JCL* 11, 215–21.

Bloom, L. Beckwith, R., Capatides, J., Hafitz, J. and Lifter, K. 1984. From infancy to language: Contributions from affect, cognition, and intentionality. Ms. New York: Teachers College, Columbia University.

Bloom, L., Bitetti Capatides, J. and Tackeff, J. 1981. Further remarks on interpretive analysis: In response to Christine Howe. *JCL* 8, 403–11.

Bloom, L., Lifter, K. and Broughton, J. 1985. The convergence of early cognition and language in the second year of life: Problems in conceptualization and measurement. In M. Barrett (ed.), *Children's Single-word Speech.* London: John Wiley.

Bloom, L., Lifter, K. and Hafitz, J. 1980. Semantics of verbs and the development of verb inflection in child language. *Language* 56, 386–412.

Bloom, L., Rocissano, L. and Hood, L. 1976. Adult-child discourse: Developmental interaction between information processing and linguistic knowledge. *Cognitive Psychology* 8, 521–52.

Bloom, L., Tackeff, J. and Lahey, M. 1984. Learning *to* in complement constructions. *JCL* 11, 391–406.

Bloomfield, L. 1933. *Language.* New York: Holt.

Blount, B. 1969. Acquisition of language by Luo children. Working paper no. 19. Berkeley: Language Behavior Research Laboratory, University of California.

Born, M. 1962. *Physics and Politics.* Edinburgh: Oliver and Boyd.

Bower, T. 1974. Repetition in human development. *Merrill-Palmer Quarterly* 20, 303–18.

Bowerman, M. 1973. *Early Syntactic Development: A cross-linguistic study with special reference to Finnish.* Cambridge: Cambridge University Press.

Braine, M. 1963. The ontogeny of English phrase structure: The first phase. *Language* 39, 1–14.

Brannigan, C. and Humphries, D. 1972. Human non-verbal behavior, a means of communication. Cited in E. Oksaar, *Language Acquisition in the Early Years: An introduction to paedolinguistics*, trans. K. Turfler. London: Batsford Academic and Educational, 1983.

Braun, C. and Klassen, B. 1971. A transformational analysis of oral syntactic structures of children representing varying ethnolinguistic communities. *Child Development* 42, 1859–71.

Braunwald, S. and Breslin, R. 1979. The diary method updated. In E. Ochs and

B. Schieffelin (eds), *Developmental Pragmatics*. New York: Academic Press.

Bretherton, I., McNew, S. Snyder, L. and Bates, E. 1983. Individual differences at 20 months: Analytic and holistic strategies in language acquisition. *JCL* 10, 293–320.

Brinton, B. and Fujiki, M. 1984. Development of topic manipulation skills in discourse. *JSHR* 27, 350–8.

Brinton, B., Fujiki, M., Loeb, D. and Winkler, E. 1986. Development of conversational repair strategies in response to requests for clarification. *JSHR* 29, 75–81.

Brown, B. and Leonard, L. 1986. Lexical influences on children's early positional patterns. *JCL* 13, 219–29.

Brown, H. 1971. Children's comprehension of relativized English sentences. *Child Development* 42, 1923–36.

Brown, R. 1957. Linguistic determinism and the parts of speech. *Journal of Abnormal Social Psychology* 55, 1–5.

—— 1966. The dialogue in early childhood. Presidential address, div. 8, American Psychological Association.

—— 1968. Derivational complexity and the order of acquisition in child speech. Carnegie-Mellon Conference on Cognitive Processes.

—— 1970. *Psycholinguistics*. New York: Free Press.

—— 1973. *A First Language: The early stages*. Cambridge, Mass.: Harvard University Press.

Brown, R., Fraser, C. and Bellugi, U. 1964. Explorations in grammar evaluation. In U. Bellugi and R. Brown (eds), *The Acquisition of Language*. Chicago: University of Chicago Press.

Bruck, M., Lambert, W. and Tucker, G. 1976. Cognitive consequences of bilingual schooling: The St. Lambert project through grade six. *International Journal of Psycholinguistics* 7, 13–33.

Bruner, J. 1975. The ontogenesis of language. *JCL* 2, 1–19.

Burmeister, H. 1982. Review of *Kommunikation unter Kindern – Methodische Reflexion und exemplarische Beschreibung*, by B. Biere. *JCL* 9, 274–6.

Carr, D. 1979. The development of young children's capacity to judge anomalous sentences. *JCL* 6, 227–41.

Carroll, J. 1964. *Language and Thought*. Englewood Cliffs, NJ: Prentice-Hall.

Carter, A. 1975. The transformation of sensorimotor morphemes into words. *JCL* 2, 233–50.

Carterette, E. and Friedman, M (eds) 1976. *Handbook of Perception. Vol. 7. Language and Speech*. New York: Academic Press.

Cartwright, C. and Cartwright, G. 1974. *Developing Observation Skills*. New York: McGraw-Hill.

Chapman, R., and Miller, J. 1973. Early two and three word utterances: Does production precede comprehension? Fifth Annual Child Language Research Forum, Stanford University.

Chapman, R., and Thomson, J. 1980. What is the source of overextension errors in comprehension testing of two-year-olds? A reply to Fremgen and Fay. *JCL* 7, 575–8.

Chipman, H., and de Dardel, C. 1974. Developmental study of the comprehension and production of the pronoun 'it' *Journal of Psycholinguistic Research* 3, 91–9.

Chomsky, C. 1969. *The Acquisition of Syntax in Children from 5 to 10*. Cambridge, Mass.: MIT Press.

Chomsky, N. 1957. *Syntactic Structures*. The Hague: Mouton.
—— 1959. Review of *Verbal behavior*, by B. Skinner. *Language* 35, 26–57.
—— 1964. Formal discussion of *The Development of Grammar in Child Language*, by W. Miller and S. Ervin. In U. Bellugi and R. Brown (eds), *The Acquisition of Language*. Chicago: University of Chicago Press.
—— 1965. *Aspects of the Theory of Syntax*. Cambridge, Mass.: MIT Press.
—— 1970. Problems of explanation in linguistics. In R. Borger and F. Cioffi (eds), *Explanation in the Behavioural Sciences*. Cambridge: Cambridge University Press.
—— 1972. *Language and Mind*. Enlarged edn. New York: Harcourt, Brace, Jovanovich.
Cicourel, A. 1974. *Cognitive Sociology: Language and meaning in social interaction*. New York: Free Press.
Cioffi, F. 1980. Freud and the idea of a pseudo-science. In R. Borger and F. Cioffi (eds), *Explanation in the Behavioural Sciences*. Cambridge: Cambridge University Press.
Clancy, P., Jacobsen, T. and Silva, M. 1976. The acquisition of conjunction: A cross-linguistic study. *PRCLD* 12, 71–80.
Clark, E. 1973. What's in a word? On the child's acquisition of semantics in his first language. In T. Moore (ed.), *Cognitive Development and the Acquisition of Language* New York: Academic Press.
Clark, E. and Berman, R. 1984. Structure and use in the acquisition of word formation. *Language* 60, 542–90.
Clark, E. and Sengul, C. 1978. Strategies in the acquisition of deixis. *JCL* 5, 457–75.
Clark, H. and Clark, E. 1977. *Psychology and Language: An introduction to psycholinguistics*. New York: Harcourt, Brace, Jovanovich.
Clark, R. 1974. Performing without competence. *JCL* 1, 1–10.
—— 1976. A report on methods of longitudinal data collection. *JCL* 3, 457–9.
Clarke, A. and Ellgring, H. 1983. Computer-aided video. In P. Dowrick and S. Biggs (eds), *Using Video*. New York: John Wiley.
Cleveland, W. 1985. *The Elements of Graphing Data*. Monterey, CA: Wadsworth.
Cleveland, W. and McGill, R. 1985. Graphical perception and graphical methods for analyzing scientific data. *Science* 229, 828–33.
Cocking, R. and McHale, S. 1981. A comparative study of the use of pictures and objects in assessing children's receptive and productive language. *JCL* 8, 1–13.
Conant, S. 1987. The relationship between age and MLU in young children. A second look at Klee and Fitzgerald's data. *JCL* 14, 169–73.
Condry, J. and Condry, S. 1976. Sex differences: a study of the eye of the beholder. *Child Development* 47, 812–19.
Cook, N. 1976. The acquisition of dimensional adjectives as a function of the underlying perceptual event. *PRCLD* 12, 81–8.
Corrigan, R. 1978. Language development as related to stage 6 object permanence development. *JCL* 5, 173–89.
Corrigan, R. and Odya-Weis, 1985. The comprehension of semantic relations by two-year-olds: An exploratory study. *JCL* 12, 47–59.
Costello, A. 1973. The reliability of direct observation. *Bulletin of the British Psychological Society* 26, 105–8.
Cox, M., and Richardson, J. 1985. How do children describe spatial relationships? *JCL* 12, 611–20.
Cromer, R. 1970. Children are nice to understand. *British Journal of Psychology* 61, 397–408.

—— 1974. Child and adult learning cues to deep structure using a picture card technique. *Journal of Psycholinguistic Research* 3, 1–14.

Cronbach, L. 1957. The two disciplines of scientific psychology. *American Psychology* 12, 671–84.

Crouch, T. 1984. Taking to the air. *Science 84*, 79–81.

Cruttenden, A. 1986. Editorial. *JCL* 13, 1–2.

Crystal, D. 1974a. Editorial. *JCL* 1, i–ii.

—— 1974b, Review of *A first language: The early stages*, by R. Brown. *JCL* 1, 289–307.

—— 1978. The analysis of intonation in young children. In F. Minifie and L. Lloyd (eds), *Communicative and Cognitive Abilities: Early behavioral assessment*. Baltimore: University Park Press.

—— 1979. *Working with LARSP*. New York: Elsevier.

Crystal. D., Fletcher, P. and Garman, M. 1976. *The Grammatical Analysis of Language Disability*. London: Edward Arnold.

Curtiss, S. 1977. *Genie: A psycholinguistic study of a modern-day 'wild child.'* New York: Academic Press.

Cziko, G. and Koda, K. 1987. A Japanese child's use of stative and punctual verbs. *JCL* 14, 99–111.

Dale, P. 1980. Is early pragmatic development measurable? *JCL* 7, 1–12.

Davidson, R., Herndon, S., Reaver, J. and Ruff, W. (eds) 1960. *The Humanities in Contemporary Life*. New York: Holt.

Davis, E. 1937. *The Development of Linguistic Skill in Twins, Singletons with Siblings, and Only Children from Age Five to Ten Years*. Minneapolis: University of Minnesota Press.

Denver, B. 1970. Representational and syntactic competence of problem readers. *Child Development* 41, 881–7.

Destefano, J. 1972. An analysis of the generative sources of prenominal adjectives in a tenth grade writing sample. *Linguistics* 92, 5–12.

Deutsch, W. 1983. How realistic is a unified theory of language acquisition? *First Language* 4, 143–56.

Dickson, W. 1980. Accuracy versus style of communication in parent–child interaction. *International Journal of Psycholinguistics* 7: 1/2, 119–30.

Donahue, M. 1986. Phonological constraints on the emergence of two-word utterances. *JCL* 13, 209–18.

Donaldson, M. 1978. *Children's Minds*. London: Fontana.

Donaldson, M. and McGarrigle, J. 1974. Some clues to the nature of semantic development. *JCL* 1, 185–94.

Dore, J. 1975. Holophrases, speech acts, and language universals. *JCL* 2, 21–40.

—— 1979. What's so conceptual about the acquisition of linguistic structures? *JCL* 6, 129–37.

Dore, J., Franklin, M., Miller, R. and Ramer, A. 1976. Transitional phenomena in early language acquisition. *JCL* 3, 13–28.

Dowrick, P. and Biggs, S. (eds) 1983. *Using Video: Psychological and social applications*. New York: John Wiley.

Dromi, E. and Berman, R. 1982. A morphemic measure of early language development: Data from modern Hebrew. *JCL* 9, 403–24.

Duchan, J. and Lund, N. 1979. Why not semantic relations? *JCL* 6, 243–51.

Dunn, J. and Kendrick, C. 1982a. *Siblings: Love, envy, and understanding.* Cambridge, Mass.: Harvard University Press.

—— 1982b. The speech of two- and three-year-olds to infant siblings: 'Baby talk' and the context of communication. *JCL* 9, 579–95.

Durkin, K. 1981. Young children's comprehension and production of novel prepositions. *International Journal of Psycholinguistics* 8:2, 31–54.

Edwards, D. and Curtiss, S. 1983. The child's conceptualization of speech and language, *First Language* 4, 41–50.

Edwards, J. 1979. Social class differences and the identification of sex in children's speech. *JCL* 6, 121–7.

Edwards, M. 1974. Perception and production in child phonology: The testing of four hypotheses. *JCL* 1, 205–19.

Ehri, L. 1976. Comprehension and production of adjectives and seriation. *JCL* 3, 369–84.

Eilers, R., Gavin, W. and Oller, D. 1982. Cross-linguistic perception in infancy: Early effects of linguistic experience. *JCL* 9, 289–302.

Eilers, R. and Oller, D. 1976. The role of speech discrimination in developmental sound substitutions. *JCL* 3, 319–29.

Eilers, R., Oller, D., Bull, D. and Gavin, W. 1984. Linguistic experience and infant speech perception: A reply to Jusczyk, Shea, and Aslin 1984. *JCL* 11, 467–75.

Eilers, R., Oller, D. and Ellington, J. 1974. The acquisition of word-meaning for dimensional adjectives: The long and short of it. *JCL* 1, 195–204.

Einstein, A. 1954. *Ideas and Opinions,* trans and rev. from *Mein Weltbild* by S. Baymann. Also other sources. New York: Dell.

Elardo, R. 1971. The experimental facilitation of children's comprehension and production of four syntactic structures. *Child Development* 42, 2101–4.

Erreich, A., Valian, V. and Winzemer, J. 1980. Aspects of a theory of language acquisition. *JCL* 7 157–79.

Ervin (-Tripp), S. 1964. Imitation and structural change in children's language. In E. Lennenberg (ed), *New Directions in the Study of Language.* Cambridge, Mass.: MIT Press.

Ervin-Tripp, S. 1974. Sociolinguistics. In B. Blount (ed), *Language, Culture and Society.* Massachusetts: Winthrop.

Eson, M., and Shapiro, A. 1982. When 'don't' means 'do': Pragmatic and cognitive development in understanding an indirect imperative. *First Language* 3, 83–91.

Fabian-Kraus, V. and Ammon, P. 1980. Assessing linguistic competence: When are children hard to understand? *JCL* 7, 401–12.

Fassnacht, G. 1982. *Theory and Practice of Observing Behavior,* trans. C. Bryant. New York: Academic Press.

Fawcett, R., and M. Perkins. 1980. *Child language transcripts 6–12,* volumes 1–4. Pontypridd, Wales: Department of Behavioural and Communication Studies, Polytechnic of Wales.

Fee, J. and Ingram, D. 1982. Reduplication as a strategy of phonological development. *JCL* 9, 41–54.

Ferguson, C. 1983. Reduplication in child phonology. *JCL* 10, 239–43.

Ferguson, C. and Farwell, C. 1975. Words and sounds in early language acquisition, *Language* 51, 419–39.

Fernald, C. 1972. Control of grammar in imitation, comprehension, and production:

Problems of replication. *Journal of Verbal Learning and Verbal Behavior* 11, 606–13.

Figueira, R. 1984. On the development of the expression of causativity: A syntactic hypothesis. *JCL* 11, 109–27.

Fillmore, C. 1968. The case for case. In E. Bach and R. Harms (eds), *Universals in Linguistic Theory*. New York: Holt, Rinehart, Winston.

Flavell, J. 1972. An analysis of cognitive developmental sequences. *Genetic Psychology Monographs* 86, 279–350.

Fletcher, P. 1981. Description and explanation in the acquisition of verb forms. *JCL* 8, 93–108.

—— 1985. *A Child's Learning of English*. Oxford: Basil Blackwell.

Flores d'Arcais, G. 1974. Review of *Il linguaggio come processo cognitivo*, by D. Parisi. *JCL* 1, 323–9.

Flynn, P. and Byrne, M. 1970. Relationship between reading and selected auditory abilities of third-grade children. *JSHR* 13, 731–40.

Fodor, J. 1968. *Psychological Explanation*. New York: Random House.

Folger, J. and Chapman, R. 1978. A pragmatic analysis of spontaneous imitations. *JCL* 5, 25–38.

Foster, S. 1986. Learning discourse topic management in the preschool years. *JCL* 13, 231–50.

Fowles, B. and Glanz, M. 1977. Competence and talent in verbal riddle comprehension. *JCL* 4, 433–52.

Francis, H. 1979. What does the child mean? A critique of the 'functional' approach to language acquisition. *JCL* 6, 201–10.

François, F., Esperet, E. and Brossard, M. 1980. Psycholinguistic analysis of the linguistic coding of a narration given by French children from different social mileux. *International Journal of Psycholinguistics* 7:3, 21–47.

Fraser, C., Bellugi, U. and Brown, R. 1963. Control of grammar in imitation, comprehension, and production. *Journal of Verbal Learning and Verbal Behavior* 2, 121–35.

Frawley, W. 1987. Review of *Handbook of Discourse Analysis* I–IV, ed. by T. van Dijk. *Language* 63, 361–97.

Freedle, R. Terrence, J. and Smith, N. 1970. Effects of mean depth and grammaticality on children's imitation of sentences. *Journal of Verbal Learning and Verbal Behavior* 9, 149–54.

Fremgen, A. and Fay, D. 1980. Overextensions in production and comprehension: A methodological clarification. *JCL* 7, 205–11.

Friend, T. and Channell, R. 1987. A comparison of two measures of receptive vocabulary. *Language, Speech, and Hearing Services in the Schools* 18, 231–7.

Fromkin, V., Krashen, S., Curtiss, S., Rigler, D. and Rigler, M. 1974. The development of language in Genie: A case of language acquisition beyond the 'critical period.' *Brain and Language* 1, 81–107.

Furrow, D. and Nelson, K. 1984. Environmental correlates of individual differences in language acquisition. *JCL* 11, 523–35.

—— 1986. A further look at the motherese hypothesis: A reply to Gleitman, Newport and Gleitman. *JCL* 13, 163–76.

Furrow, D., Nelson, K. and Benedict, H. 1979. Mothers' speech to children and syntactic development: Some simple relationships. *JCL* 6, 423–42.

Galligan, R. 1987. Intonation with single words: Purposive and grammatical use. *JCL* 14, 1–21.

Gans, E. 1981. *The Origin of Language: A formal theory of representation.* Berkeley: University of California Press.

Garnica, O. 1977. Some prosodic and paralinguistic features of speech to young children. In C. Snow and C. Ferguson (eds), *Talking to Children. Language Input and Acquisition.* Cambridge: Cambridge University Press.

Gathercole, V. 1983. The mass-count distinction: Children's uses of morpho-syntactic vs. semantic approaches. *PRCLD* 22, 58–65.

—— 1986. The acquisition of the present perfect: Explaining differences in the speech of Scottish and American children. *JCL* 13, 537–60.

van der Geest, A. 1974. *Evaluation of Theories on Child Grammars.* The Hague: Mouton.

Gelfand, D. and Hartmann, D. 1984. *Child Behavior Analysis and Therapy*, 2nd edn. Oxford: Pergamon Press.

Gelso, C. 1973. Effect of audiorecording and videorecording on client satisfaction and self-expression. *Journal of Consultative and Clinical Psychology* 40, 455–61.

Gewirtz, J. and Boyd, E. 1976. *Mother–infant Interaction and its Study.* Vol. 11 of H. Reese (ed), *Advances in Child Development and Behavior.* New York: Academic Press.

Gilbert, J. and Johnson, C. 1978. Temporal and sequential constraints on six-year-olds' phonological productions: Some observations on the 'ambliance' phenomenon. *JCL* 5, 101–12.

Gleitman, L., Gleitman, H. and Shipley, E. 1972. The emergence of the child as grammarian. *Cognition* 1, 137–64.

Gleitman, L., Newport, E. and Gleitman, H. 1984. The current status of the motherese hypothesis. *JCL* 11, 43–79.

Gleitman, L. Shipley, E. and Smith, C. 1978. Old and new ways not to study comprehension: Comments on Petretic and Tweney's (1977) experimental review of Shipley, Smith and Gleitman (1969). *JCL* 5, 501–19.

de Gòes, C. and Martlew, M. 1983. Beginning to read and write: An exploratory study of young children's understanding of metalinguistic terms and graphic conventions. *First Language* 4, 121–30.

Goldman-Eisler, F. 1972. What should be the methods in psycholinguistics? *International Journal of Psycholinguistics* 1, 68–73.

Golinkoff, R. and Gordon, L. 1987. Review of *Language Development in the Preschool Years*, by G. Wells. *JCL* 14, 179–200.

Gopnik, A. 1984. The acquisition of *gone* and the development of the object concept. *JCL* 11, 273–92.

Grace, J. and Suci, G. 1985. Attentional priority in the acquisition of word reference. *JCL* 12, 1–12.

Greenfield, P. 1980. Going beyond information theory to explain early word choice: A reply to Roy Pea. *JCL* 7, 217–21.

—— 1982. The role of perceived variability in the transition to language. *JCL* 9, 1–12.

Greenfield P. and Smith, J. 1976. *The Structure of Communication in Early Language Development.* New York: Academic Press.

Guess, D. 1969. A functional analysis of receptive language and productive speech: Acquisition of the plural morpheme, *Journal of Applied Behavior Analysis* 2, 255–64.

Guess, D. and Baer, D. 1973. An analysis of individual differences in generalization between receptive and productive language in retarded children. *Journal of Applied Behavior Analysis* 6, 311–29.

Guillaume, P. 1927. Les débuts de la phrase dans le langage de l'enfant. *Journal de Psychologie* 24, 1–25.

Gullo, D. 1982. A developmental study of low- and middle-class children's responses to WH-questions. *First Language* 3, 211–21.

Halliday, M. 1975. *Learning How to Mean.* London: Edward Arnold.

Hart, B. 1975. The use of adult cues to test the language competence of young children. *JCL* 2, 105–24.

Haviland, S. and Clark, E. 1974. 'This man's father is my father's son'. A study of the acquisition of English kin terms. *JCL* 1, 23–47.

van Hekken, S. and Roelofsen, W. 1982. More questions than answers: A study of question-answer sequences in a naturalistic setting. *JCL* 9, 445–60.

Hockett, C. 1958. *A Course in Modern Linguistics.* New York: Macmillan.

Hoff-Ginsberg, E. 1985. Some contributions of mothers' speech to their children's syntactic growth. *JCL* 12, 367–85.

Holzman, M. 1972. The use of interrogative forms in the verbal interaction of three mothers and their children. *Journal of Psycholinguistic Research* 1, 311–36.

Homans, G. 1967. *The Nature of Social Science.* New York: Harvest/Harcourt, Brace, Jovanovich.

Hornby, P. and Hass, W. 1970. Use of contrastive stress by preschool children. *JSHR* 13, 395–9.

Houston, S. 1972, Child Black English: The school register. *Linguistics* 90, 20–34.

—— 1973. Syntactic complexity and information transmission in first-graders: A cross-cultural study. *Journal of Psycholinguistic Research* 2, 99–114.

Howe, C. 1976. The meanings of two-word utterances in the speech of young children. *JCL* 3, 29–47.

Hughes, S. and Walsh, J. 1971. Effects of syntactical mediation, age, and modes of representation on paired-associate learning. *Child Development*, 42, 1827–36.

Huttenlocher, J. 1974. The origins of language comprehension. In R. Solso (ed), *Theories in Cognitive Psychology.* Potomac, Maryland: Erlbaum.

Huttenlocher, J. and Weiner, S. 1971. Comprehension of instructions in varying contexts. *Cognitive Psychology* 2, 369–85.

Hyams, N. 1984. The acquisition of infinitival complements: A reply to Bloom, Tackeff and Lahey. *JCL* 11, 679–83.

Ingram D. 1971. Transitivity in child language. *Language* 47, 888–910.

—— 1972. The acquisition of questions and its relation to cognitive development in normal and linguistically deviant children: A pilot study. *PRCLD* 4, 13–8.

—— 1974. The relationship between comprehension and production. In R. Schiefelbusch and L. Lloyd (eds), *Language Perspectives: Acquisition, retardation and intervention.* Baltimore: University Park Press.

—— 1981. *Procedures for the Phonological Analysis of Children's Language.* Baltimore: University Park Press.

Irwin, D. 1952. Speech development in the young child: 2. Some factors related to the speech development of the infant and young child. *JSHD* 17, 269–79.

Jakobson, R. 1969. *The Paths from Infancy to Language.* Heinz Werner Lectures, Clark University, Worcester, Massachusetts.

James, S. and Miller, J. 1973. Children's awareness of semantic constraints in sentences. *Child Development* 44, 69–76.

Jarovinskij, A. 1979. On the lexical competence of bilingual children of kindergarten age groups. *International Journal of Psycholinguistics* 6:3, 43–57.

Jarvie, I. 1970. Understanding and explanation in sociology and social anthropology. In R. Borger and F. Cioffi (eds), *Explanation in the Behavioural Sciences* Cambridge: Cambridge University Press.

Johnson, C. and Bush, C. 1970. Note on transcribing the speech of young children. *PRCLD* 1.

Johnson, J. 1984. Acquisition of locative meanings: *Behind* and *in front of. JCL* 11, 407–22.

Johnson, S. and Bolstadt, O. 1972. Methodological issues in naturalistic observation: Some problems and solutions for field research. Proceedings of the Banff Conference. Champaign, Illinois: Research Press.

Josephson, J. and Destefano, J. 1979. An analysis of productive control over an educational register in school age children's language. *International Journal of Psycholinguistics* 6:4, 41–55.

Judson, H. 1984. Century of the sciences. *Science 84*, 41–3.

Jusczyk, P., Shea, S. and Aslin, R. 1984. Linguistic experience and infant speech perception: A re-examination of Eilers, Gavin and Oller 1982. *JCL* 11, 453–66.

Kamhi, A. 1982. Overextensions and underextensions: How different are they? *JCL* 9, 243–7.

—— 1985. Questioning the value of large *N*, multivariate studies: A response to Schery (1985). Letter. *JSHD* 10, 288–90.

Kaplan, L. 1978. *Oneness and Separateness: From infant to individual.* New York: Simon and Schuster.

Kaplan, M. 1984. *Science, Language, and the Human Condition.* New York: Paragon House.

Kay, D. and Anglin, J. 1982. Overextension and underextension in the child's expressive and receptive speech. *JCL* 9, 83–98.

Keenan (Ochs), E. and Klein, E. 1975. Coherency in children's discourse. *Journal of Psycholinguistic Research* 4, 365–80.

Kelleher, T. 1973. Testing, teaching, and retesting syntactic structures in children from 5 to 10 *Linguistics* 115, 15–38.

Kenney, K. and Prather, E. 1986. Articulation development in preschool children: Consistency of productions. *JSHR* 29, 29–36.

Kessen, W. 1960. Research design in the study of developmental problems. In P. Mussen (ed), *Handbook of Research Methods in Child Development.* New York: John Wiley.

Klecan-Aker, J. 1984. A study of the syntactic skills of normal middle-school males and females. *Language and Speech* 27, 205–15.

Klee, T. 1985. Role of inversion in children's question development. *JSHR* 28, 225–32.

Klee, T. and Fitzgerald, M. 1985. The relation between grammatical development and mean length of utterance in morphemes. *JCL* 12, 251–69.

Klein, H. 1984. Learning to stress: A case study. *JCL* 11, 375–90.

Knafle, J. 1974. Children's discrimination of rhyme *JSHR* 17, 367–72.

Kornfeld, J. n.d. Theoretical issues in child phonology. Ms. Cambridge, Mass.: MIT Research Laboratory of Electronics.

Koster, J. and May, R. 1982. On the constituency of infinitives. *Language* 58, 116–43.

Kuhn, T. 1970. *The Structure of Scientific Revolutions.* Vol. 2, no. 2 of *International Encyclopedia of Unified Science*, 2nd edn. Chicago: University of Chicago Press.

Labov, W. 1971. Methodology. In W. Dingwall (ed.), *A Survey of Linguistic Science.* University of Maryland Linguistics Program.

de Laguna, G. 1927. *Speech: Its function and development.* New Haven: Yale University Press.

Landsmann, L. and Levin, I. 1987. Writing in four-to-six-year-olds: Representation of semantic and phonetic similarities and differences. *JCL* 14, 127–44.

Lee, L. 1966. Developmental sentence types: A method for comparing normal and deviant syntactic development. *JSHD* 31, 311–30.

—— 1974. *Developmental Sentence Analysis*. Evanston, Illinois: Northwestern University Press.

Lee, L. and Canter, S. 1971. Developmental sentence scoring: A clinical procedure for estimating syntactic development in children's spontaneous speech. *JSHD* 36, 315–40.

Leech, G. 1983. *Principles of Pragmatics*. London: Longman.

Lefebvre-Pinard, M., Vézina, L., Bouffard-Bouchard, T. and Strayer, F. 1980. Social cognition and dyadic communication among preschool children. *International Journal of Psycholinguistics* 7:1/2, 59–67.

Lehmann, W. 1987. President's column: Language, linguistics, and the Modern Language Association. MLA Newsletter 19–2.

Lempert, H. and Kinsbourne, M. 1980. Preschool children's sentence comprehension: Strategies with respect to word order. *JCL* 7, 371–80.

Lengyel, Z. 1977. Development of parts of speech in the Hungarian child language. *International Journal of Psycholinguistics* 4:1, 51–65.

Leonard, L. Schwartz R., Folger, M. and Wilcox, M. 1978. Some aspects of child phonology in imitative and spontaneous speech. *JCL* 5, 403–15.

Leopold, W. 1939. 1947. 1949a. 1949b. *Speech Development of a Bilingual Child*, vols I–IV. Evanston, Illinois: Northwestern University Press.

—— 1948. The study of child language and infant bilingualism. *Word* 4, 173–80.

Levine, S. and Carey, S. 1982. Up front: The acquisition of a concept and a word. *JCL* 9, 645–57.

Lewis, M. 1951. *Infant Speech: A study of the beginnings of language*. New York: Humanities Press.

—— 1972. Culture and gender roles: There is no unisex in the nursery. *Psychology Today* 5, 54–7.

Lewis, M. and Cherry, L. 1977. Social behavior and language acquisition. In M. Lewis and L. Rosenblum (eds), *Interaction, Conversation, and the Development of Language*. New York: John Wiley.

Lewis, M. and Lee-Painter, S. 1975. The origin of interactions: Methodological issues. In K. Riegel and G. Rosenwald (eds), *Structure and Transformation: Developmental and historical aspects*. New York: John Wiley.

Li, C. and Thompson, S. 1977. The acquisition of tone in Mandarin-speaking children. *JCL* 4, 185–99.

Liles, B. 1985. Cohesion in the narratives of normal and language-disordered children. *JSHR* 28, 123–33.

Limber, J. 1976. Unraveling competence, performance and pragmatics in the speech of young children. *JCL* 3, 309–18.

Ling, D. and Ling, A. 1974. Communication development in the first three years of life. *JSHD* 17, 159–64.

Lingquest Software, Inc. 1982. Promotional brochure.

Lively, M. 1984. Developmental sentence scoring: Common scoring errors. *Language Speech, and Hearing Services in the Schools* 15, 154–68.

Livingston, D. 1953. *Film and the Director*. New York: Macmillan.

Lloyd, P. and Donaldson, M. 1976. On a method of eliciting true/false judgments from young children. *JCL* 3, 411–16.

Local, J. 1983. How many vowels in a vowel? *JCL* 10, 449–53.

Lock, A. and Fisher, E. (eds) 1984. *Language Development*. London: Croom Helm.

Long, S. 1986. *Computerized profiling*. Arcata, California: Computerized Profiling.

Lovell, K. and Dixon, E. 1967. The growth of the control of grammar in imitation, comprehension, and production. *Journal of Child Psychology and Psychiatry* 8, 31–9.

Lowell, E. Curtiss, S., Bennett(-Kastor), T., Prutting, C., Rouin, C. and Dunlea, A. 1977. A search for performatives in young deaf children. Final report submitted to the Spencer Foundation.

Luján, M., Minaya, L. and Sankoff, D. 1984. The universal consistency hypothesis and the prediction of word order acquisition stages in the speech of bilingual children. *Language* 60, 343–71.

Lykken, D. 1968. Statistical significance in psychological research. *Psychology Review* 70, 151–9.

Lynch, J. 1983. Gender differences in language. *ASHA* 25, 37–42.

Macaulay, R. 1978. The myth of female superiority in language. *JCL* 5, 353–63.

McCall, R. 1977. Challenges to a science of developmental, psychology. *Child Development* 48, 333–44.

McCauley, R. and Skenes, L. 1987. Contrastive stress, phonetic context, and misarticulation of /r/ in young children. *JSHR* 30, 114–21.

Mack, M. and Lieberman, P. 1985. Acoustic analysis of words produced by a child from 46 to 149 weeks. *JCL* 12, 527–50.

MacKain, K. 1982. Assessing the role of experience on infants' speech discrimination. *JCL* 9, 527–42.

Macken, M. 1979. Developmental reorganization of phonology: A hierarchy of basic units of acquisition. *Lingua* 49, 11–49.

Macken, M. and Barton, D. 1977. A longitudinal study of the acquisition of the voicing contrast in American-English word-initial stops, as measured by voice onset time. *PRCLD* 14, 74–120.

—— 1980a. The acquisition of the voicing contrast in English: A study of voice onset time in word-initial stop consonants. *JCL* 7, 41–74.

—— 1980b. The acquisition of the voicing contrast in Spanish: A phonetic and phonological study of word-initial stop consonants. *JCL* 7, 433–58.

McNeill, D. 1966. Developmental psycholinguistics. In F. Smith and G. Miller (eds), *The Genesis of Language*. Cambridge, Mass.: MIT Press.

—— 1970. *The Acquisition of Language: The study of developmental psycholinguistics*. New York: Harper and Row.

McNeill, D. Yukawa, R. and McNeill, N. 1971. The acquisition of direct and indirect objects in Japanese. *Child Development* 42, 237–49.

McReynolds, L.V. and Kearns, K. 1983. *Single-subject Experimental Designs in Communication Disorders*. Baltimore: University Park Press.

McTear, M. 1978. Review of *Talking to children: Language input and acquisition*, ed. by C. Snow and C. Ferguson. *JCL* 5, 521–30.

MacWhinney, B. 1975. Rules, rote, and analogy in morphological formations by Hungarian children. *JCL* 2, 65–77.

—— 1983. Review of *Language acquisition and linguistic theory*, ed. by S. Tavakolian. *JCL* 10, 667–72.

MacWhinney, B. and Snow, C. 1985. The child language data exchange system. *JCL* 12, 271–96.

Mahler, M., Pines, F. and Bergman, A. 1975. *The Psychological Birth of the Human*

Infant: Symbiosis and individuation. New York: Basic Books.

Maratsos, M. 1974. Children who get worse at understanding the passive: 9 replications of Bever. *Journal of Psycholinguistic Research* 3, 65–74.

Martin, J. and Molfese, D. 1972. Preferred adjective ordering in very young children. *Journal of Verbal Learning and Verbal Behavior* 11, 287–92.

Matthei, E. 1987. Subject and agent in emerging grammars: Evidence for a change in children's baises. *JCL* 14, 295–308.

Matthews, P. 1975. Review of *A First Language: The early years*, by R. Brown. *Journal of Linguistics* 11, 322–43.

—— 1983. Review of *Explanation in Linguistics: The logical problem of language acquisition*, ed. by N. Hornstein and D. Lightfoot. *JCL* 10, 491–3.

Maxwell, G. and Pringle, J. 1983. The analysis of video records. In P. Dowrick and S. Biggs (eds), *Using Video: Psychological and social applications.* New York: John Wiley.

Meng, K. 1981. Verbal-communicative performance of preschool children in a cooperative setting. *International Journal of Psycholinguistics* 8:4, 105–19.

Menn, L. 1982. Discussant's remarks: Methodological considerations in studying the acquisition of intonation contour. *PRCLD* 21, 134–6.

Merleau-Ponty, M. 1973. *Consciousness and the Acquisition of Language*, trans. H. Silverman. Evanston, Illinois: Northwestern University Press.

Mervis, C. and Canada, K. 1983. On the existence of competence errors in early comprehension: A reply to Fremgen and Fay and Chapman and Thomson. *JCL* 10, 431–40.

Miller, J. and Chapman, R. 1983. A computer solution to free speech sample analysis. Miniseminar presented at the Annual Convention of the American Speech-Language-Hearing Association, Cincinnati, Ohio.

Moerk, E. 1974. A design for multivariate analysis of language behavior and language development. *Language and Speech* 17, 240–54.

—— 1975. The multiple channels of the young child's communicative behavior. *Linguistics* 160, 21–32.

—— 1977. *Pragmatic and Semantic Aspects of Early Language Development.* Baltimore: University Park Press.

—— 1980. Relationship between parental input frequencies and children's language acquisition: A reanalysis of Brown's data. *JCL* 7, 105–18.

Morehead, D. 1971. Processing of phonological sequences by young children and adults. *Child Development* 42, 279–89.

Morra Pellegrino, M. and Andreani Scopesi, A. 1978. Oral and written language in children: Syntactical development of descriptive language. *International Journal of Psycholinguistics* 5:1, 5–19.

Morsbach, G. and Steel, P. 1976. 'John is easy to see' reinvestigated. *JCL* 3, 443–7.

Moskowitz, A. 1970. The two-year-old stage in the acquisition of English phonology. *Language* 46, 426–41.

Mussen, P. (ed) 1960. *Handbook of Research Methods in Child Development.* New York: John Wiley.

Nakayama, M. 1987. Performance factors in subject-auxiliary inversion by children. *JCL* 14, 113–25.

Nelson, K. 1973. Structure and strategy in learning to talk. *Monographs of the Society for Research in Child Development* 38, nos. 1–2, serial no. 149.

Nelson, K. and Benedict, H. 1974. The comprehension of relative, absolute, and contrastive adjectives by young children. *Journal of Psycholinguistic Research* 3, 333–42.

Newmeyer, F. 1986a. Has there been a 'Chomskyan revolution' in linguistics? *Language* 62, 1–18.

—— 1986b. *Linguistic Theory in America*, 2nd edn. New York: Academic Press.

Newport, E. Gleitman, H. and Gleitman, L. 1977. Mother, I'd rather do it myself: Some effects and non-effects of maternal speech style. In C. Snow and C. Ferguson (eds), *Talking to Children: Language input and acquisition*. Cambridge: Cambridge University Press.

Ochs, E. 1979. Transcription as theory. In E. Ochs and B. Schieffelin (eds), *Developmental Pragmatics*. New York: Academic Press.

—— 1982. Ergativity and word order in Samoan child language. *Language* 58, 646–71.

Oksaar, E. 1983. *Language Acquisition in the Early Years: An introduction to paedolinguistics*, trans. K. Turfler. London: Batsford Academic and Educational.

Oller, D. and Eilers, R. 1982. Similarity of babbling in English-and Spanish-learning babies. *JCL* 9, 565–77.

Olney, R. and Scholnick, E. 1978. An experimental investigation of adult perception of one-word utterances. *JCL* 5, 131–42.

Olsen-Fulero, L. and Conforti, J. 1983. Child responsiveness to mother questions of varying type and presentation. *JCL* 10, 495–520.

Osgood, C. and Sebeok, T. (eds) 1965. *Psycholinguistics: A survey of theory and research problems*. Bloomington: Indiana University Press.

Parisi, D. and Giannelli, W. 1979. Language and social environment at 2 years. *Merrill-Palmer Quarterly* 25, 61–75.

Pea, R. 1979. Can information theory explain early word choice? *JCL* 6, 397–410.

Pellegrini, A. 1980. A semantic analysis of preschoolers' self-regulating speech. *International Journal of Psycholinguistics* 7:4, 59–74.

Pellegrini, A. and Destefano, J. 1979. The functions of private speech in preschool children. *International Journal of Psycholinguistics* 6:3, 27–42.

Percival, W.K. 1976. The applicability of Kuhn's paradigms to the history of linguistics. *Language* 52, 285–94.

Perlmutter, D. 1980. Relational Grammar. In E. Moravcsik and J. Wirth (eds), *Current Approaches to Syntax*, vol. 13 of *Syntax and Semantics*. New York: Academic Press.

Pertz, D. and Bever, T. 1975. Sensitivity to phonological universals in children and adolescents. *Language* 51, 149–62.

Peters, A. 1977. Language learning strategies:. Does the whole equal the sum of the parts? *Language* 53, 560–73.

Petretic, P. and Tweney, R. 1977. Does comprehension precede production? The development of children's responses to telegraphic sentences of varying grammatical adequacy. *JCL* 4, 201–9.

Piaget, J. 1950. *The Psychology of Intelligence*. London: Routledge and Kegan Paul.

—— 1972. *The Epistemology of Interdisciplinary Relationship. Interdisciplinarity, problems of teaching and research in universities*. Paris: OECD (CERI).

Pike, K. 1967. *Language in Relation to a Unified Theory of Human Behavior*. The Hague: Mouton.

Pinker, S. 1979. Formal models of language learning. *Cognition* 7, 217–83.

Platt, C. and MacWhinney, B. 1983. Error assimilation as a mechanism in language learning. *JCL* 10, 401–14.

Platt, M. 1983. Deictic particles in Samoan child language. *PRCLD* 22, 116–23.

Pollio, M. and Pollio, H. 1974. The development of figurative language in children. *Journal of Psycholinguistic Research* 3, 185–202.

Powers, M. 1971. Functional disorders of articulation: Symptomatology and etiology. In L. Travis (ed.), *Handbook of Speech Pathology and Audiology*. New York: Appleton-Century Crofts.

Pratt, C., Tunmer, W., and Bowey, H. 1984. Children's capacity to correct grammatical violations in sentences. *JCL* 11, 129–41

Preece, A. 1987. The range of narrative forms conversationally produced by young children. *JCL* 14, 353–73.

Presson, C. 1982. Understanding sentences in varying contexts. *JCL* 9, 217–28.

Prideaux, G. 1985. *Psycholinguistics: The experimental study of language*. New York: Guilford.

Priestly, T. 1977. One idiosyncratic strategy in the acquisition of phonology, *JCL* 4, 45–65.

—— 1980. Homonymy in child phonology. *JCL* 7, 413–27.

Przetacznikowa, M. 1977. The development of attributive relations in child language. *International Journal of Psycholinguistics* 4:2, 43–59.

Quirk, R., Greenbaum, S., Leech, G. and Svartik, J. 1972. *A Grammar of Contemporary English*. London: Longman.

Raffin, M. 1986. A response to Kamhi's (1985) 'Questioning the value of large *N*, multivariate studies: A response to Schery (1985).' *JSHD* 51, 94.

Ramer, A. 1976. Syntactic styles in emerging language. *JCL* 3, 49–62.

Ramer A. and Rees, M. 1973. Selected aspects of the development of English morphology in Black American children of low socio-economic background. *JSHR* 16, 569–77.

Randall, T. 1976. An analysis of observer influence on sex and social class differences in mother-infant interaction. ERIC Reports, ed. no. 114204.

Renne, C., Dowrick, P. and Wasek, G. 1983. Considerations of the participant in video recording. In P. Dowrick and S. Biggs (eds), *Using Video: Psychological and social applications*. New York: John Wiley.

Rescorla, L. 1981. Category development in early language. *JCL* 8, 225–38.

Retherford, K., Schwartz, B. and Chapman, R. 1981. Semantic roles and residual grammatical categories in mother and child speech: Who tunes in to whom? *JCL* 8, 583–608.

Richards, B. 1987. Type/token ratios: What do they really tell us? *JCL* 14, 201–9.

Ringel, R., Trachtman, L. and Prutting, C. 1984. The science in human communication sciences. *ASHA* 26:12, 33–7.

Rispoli, M. and Bloom, L. 1985. Incomplete and continuing: Theoretical issues in the acquisition of tense and aspect. *JCL* 12, 471–4.

Rival, I. 1987. Picture puzzling. *The Sciences* 27:1, 40–6.

Rodgon, M. 1977. Situation and meaning in one- and two-word utterances: Observations on Howe's 'The meanings of two-word utterances in the speech of young children.' *JCL* 4, 111–14.

Rosch, E. 1973. On the internal structure of perceptual and semantic categories. In T. Moore (ed.), *Cognitive Development and the Acquisition of Language*. New York: Academic Press.

Rosenberg, S., Jarvella, R. and Cross, M. 1971. Semantic integration, age, and the recall of sentences. *Child Development* 42, 1959–66.

Rosenthal, D. 1979. Language skills and formal operations. *Merrill-Palmer Quarterly* 25, 133–43.

Rosenthal, M. 1973. The study of infant–environment interaction: Some comments on trends and methodologies. *Journal of Child Psychology and Psychiatry* 14, 301–17.

Roth, F. 1984. Accelerating language learning in young children. *JCL* 11, 89–107.

Rubin, D. 1982, Adapting syntax in writing to varying audiences as a function of age and social cognitive ability. *JCL* 9, 497–510.

Ruder, K. Smith, M. and Murai, H. 1980. Response to commands revisited again. *JCL* 7, 197–203.

Ruke-Dravina, V. 1976 'Mama' and 'papa' in child language. *JCL* 3, 157–66.

Ryan, E. and Ledger, G. 1979. Grammaticality judgments, sentence repetitions, and sentence corrections of children learning to read. *International Journal of Psycholinguistics* 6:4, 23–40.

Sabeau-Jouannet, E. 1978. A study of syntactic and semantic aspects of dialogues between young children. *International Journal of Psycholinguistics* 5:4, 39–54.

Saltz, E., Soller, E. and Sigel, I. 1972. The development of natural language concepts. *Child Development* 43, 1191–202.

Savić, S. and Jocić, M. 1975. Some features of dialogue between twins. *International Journal of Psycholinguistics* 4, 33–51.

Scarborough, H., Wyckoff, J. and Davidson, R. 1986. A reconsideration of the relation between age and mean utterance length. *JSHR* 29, 394–9.

Schaerlaekens, A. 1973. *The Two-word Sentence in Child Language Development: A study based on evidence provided by Dutch-speaking triplets.* The Hague: Mouton.

Scheflen, A., Kendon, A. and Schaeffer, J. 1970. On the choices of audiovisual media. In M. Berger (ed.), *Videotape Techniques in Psychiatric Training and Treatment* New York: Brunner/Mazel.

Schieffelin, B. 1979. Getting it together: An ethnographic approach to the study of the development of communicative competence. In E. Ochs and B. Schieffelin (eds), *Developmental Pragmatics.* New York: Academic Press.

Schlesinger, I. 1971a. Learning grammar: From pivot to realization rule. In R. Huxley and E. Ingram (eds), *Language Acquisition: Models and methods.* New York: Academic Press.

—— 1971b. Production of utterances and language acquisition. In D. Slobin (ed.), *The Ontogenesis of Grammar* New York: Academic Press.

—— 1977. The role of cognitive development and linguistic input in language acquisition. *JCL* 153–69.

Schloon, M. 1976. Dissertation Univesity of Hamburg. Cited in E. Oksaar, *Language Acquisition in the Early Years: An introduction to paedolinguistics,* trans. K. Turfler. London: Batsford Academic and Educational.

Scholes, R. 1970. On functors and connectives in children's imitations of word strings. *Journal of Verbal Learning and Verbal Behavior* 9, 167–70.

Schwartz, R. 1984. Words, objects, and actions in early lexical acquisition. *JSHR* 27, 119–27.

Schwartz, R. and Camarata, S. 1985. Examining relationships between input and language development: Some statistical issues. *JCL* 12, 199–207.

Schwartz, R., Chapman, K., Prelock, P., Terrell, B. and Rowan, L. 1985. Facilitation of early syntax through discourse structure. *JCL* 12, 13–25.

Schwartz, R. and Leonard, L. 1983. Some further comments on reduplication in child phonology. *JCL* 10, 441–8.

Schwartz, R., Leonard, L., Wilcox, M. and Folger, K. 1980. Again and again: Reduplication in child phonology. *JCL* 7, 75–88.

Scollon, R. 1974. Dissertation University of Hawaii. One child's language from one to two: The origins of construction.

—— 1976. *Conversations with a One-year-old.* Honolulu: University of Hawaii Press.

—— 1979. A real early stage: An unzippered condensation of a disseration of child language. In E. Ochs and B. Schieffelin (eds), *Developmental Pragmatics*. New York: Academic Press.

Shipley, E., Smith, C. and Gleitman, L. 1969. A study in the acquisition of language: Free responses to commands. *Language* 45, 322–43.

Shriner, T. and Daniloff, R. 1970. Reassembly of segmented CVC syllables by children. *JSHR* 13, 537–47.

Shugar, G. 1978. Peer face-to-face interactions at ages three to five. *International Journal of Psycholinguistics* 5:4, 17–37.

—— 1981. Early child discourse analysed in the dyadic interaction unit. *International Journal of Psycholinguistics* 8:2, 55–78.

Siegel, G. and Young M. 1987. Group designs in clinical research. *JSHD* 52, 194–9.

Silverman, E. -M. 1973. Clustering: A characteristic of preschoolers' speech disfluency. *JSHR* 16, 578–83.

Simpson, R. 1985. A schema of science. Review of *The Intellectual and Social Organization of the Sciences*, by R. Whitely. *Science* 230, 658–9.

Sinclair, A. 1980. Thinking about language: An interview study of children aged three to eight. *International Journal of Psycholinguistics* 7:4, 19–40.

—— 1981. Children's judgments of inappropriate speech acts. *International Journal of Psycholinguistics* 8:3, 75–94.

Skinner, B. 1957. *Verbal Behavior*. New York: Appleton-Century-Crofts.

Slama-Cazacu, T. 1966. Essay on psycholinguistic methodology and some of its applications. *Linguistics* 24, 51–72.

—— 1972a. Fifty years of European child language studies, and perspectives in this field. Colloquium paedolinguisticum, Proceedings of First International Symposium of Paedolinglinguistics, Brno, 1970. The Hague: Mouton.

—— 1972b. The study of child language in Europe. In T. Sebeok (ed.), *Current Trends in Linguistics*, vol. 9. The Hague: Mouton.

—— 1980. A psycholinguistic approach to the study of communication in various milieux. *International Journal of Psycholinguistics* 7:1/2, 105–17.

Slobin, D. 1970. Universals of grammatical development in children. In W. Levelt and G. Flores d'Arcais (eds), *Advances in Psycholinguistic Research*. Amsterdam: North Holland.

Slobin, D. and Welsh, C. 1973. Elicited imitation as a research tool in developmental psycholinguistics. In C. Ferguson and D. Slobin (eds), *Studies of Child Language Development* New York: Holt, Rinehart and Winston.

Smith, C. 1980. The acquisition of time talk: Relations between child and adult grammars. *JCL* 7, 263–78.

Smith, C. and Weist, R. 1987. On the temporal contour of child language: A reply to Rispoli and Bloom. *JCL* 387–92.

Snow, C. 1977. The development of conversation between mothers and babies. *JCL* 4, 1–22.

Snow, C. and Ferguson, C. 1977. *Talking to Children. Language input and acquisition*. Cambridge: Cambridge University Press.

Snow, C. and Goldfield, B. 1983. Turn the page please: Situation-specific language acquisition. *JCL* 10, 551–69.

Snow, C., Smith, N. and Hoefnagel-Höhle, M. 1980. The acquisition of some Dutch morphological rules. *JCL* 7, 539–53.

Stern, C., and Bryson, J. 1970. Competence versus performance in young children's use of adjectival comparatives. *Child Development* 41, 1197–201.

Stern, C., and Stern, W. 1907. *Die Kindersprache*. 4th rev. edn, 1928. Leipzig: Barth.

Stern, W. 1930. *Psychology of Early Childhood: Up to the sixth year of age*, trans. A. Barwell. 2nd edn. London: Allen and Unwin.

Stern, W. and Stern, C. 1907. Anleitung zur Beobachtung der Sprachentwicklung bei normalen vollsinnigen Kindern. *Zeitschrift für Angewandte Psychologie* 2, 313–37.

Stewart, J. and Sinclair, H. 1975. Comprehension of questions by children between 5 and 9. *International Journal of Psycholinguistics* 3, 17–26.

Straight, H. 1979. A redefinition of the relationship between psycholinguistics and linguistics? *International Journal of Psycholinguistics* 6:4, 57–60.

—— 1980. Cognitive development and communicative interaction as determinants of the emerging language abilities of children. Article reviewing four books. *International Journal of Psycholinguistics* 7:1/2, 143–67.

Strage, A. 1982. The expression of contrast in child discourse. *PRCLD* 21, 95–103.

Summerfield, A. 1983. Recording social interaction. In P. Dowrick and S. Biggs (eds), *Using Video: Psychological and social interactions*. New York: John Wiley.

Surian, L. and Job, R. 1987. Children's use of conversational rules in a referential communication task. *Journal of Psycholinguistic Research* 16, 369–82.

Tamil, L. 1979. Language development: New directions. *Human Development* 22, 263–9. Reprinted in A. Lock and E. Fisher (eds), *Language Development*. London: Croom Helm, 1984.

Taylor, C. 1970. The explanation of purposive behavior. In R. Borger and F. Cioffi (eds), *Explanation in the Behavioural Sciences*. Cambridge: Cambridge University Press.

Templin, M. 1957. *Certain Language Skills in Children*. Minneapolis: University of Minnesota Press.

von Tetzchner, S. and Martinsen, H. 1980. A psycholinguistic study of the language of the blind: 1. Verbalism. *International Journal of Psycholinguistics* 7:3, 49–61.

Thieman, T. 1975. Imitation and recall of optionally deletable sentences by young children. *JCL* 2, 261–9.

Thomson, J. and Chapman, R. 1977. Who is 'Daddy' revisited: The status of two-year-olds' over-extended words in use and comprehension. *JCL* 4, 359–75.

Titone, R. 1980. Psycholinguistic variables of child bilingualism: Cognition and personality development. *International Journal of Psycholinguistics* 7:3, 5–19.

Tomasello, M. and Farrar, M. 1984. Cognitive bases of lexical development: Object permanence and relational words. *JCL* 11, 477–94.

Toulmin, S. 1970. Reasons and causes. In R. Borger and F. Cioffi (eds), *Explanation in the Behavioural Sciences*. Cambridge: Cambridge University Press.

Tse, S.-M. and Ingram, D. 1987. The influence of dialectal variation on phonological acquisition: A case study on the acquisition of Cantonese. *JCL* 14, 281–94.

Tversky, A. and Kahneman, D. 1971. Belief in the law of small numbers. *Psychology Bulletin* 76, 105–10.

Tweney, R., and Petretic, P. 1981. On the comprehension of comprehension studies: A reply to Gleitman, Shipley and Smith's (1978) criticism of Petretic and Tweney

(1977). *JCL* 8, 193–204.

Tyack, D. and Ingram, D. 1977. Children's production and comprehension of questions. *JCL* 4, 211–24.

Understanding science, technology and society: An interdisciplinary approach. 1985. *LAS Newsletter*. Urbana, Illinois: University of Illinois.

Vanevery, K. and Rosenberg, S. 1970. Semantics, phrase structure, and age as variables in sentence recall. *Child Development* 41, 835–9.

Velten, H. 1943. The growth of phonemic and lexical patterns in infant language. *Language* 19, 281–92.

Veneziano, E. 1981. Early language and nonverbal representation: A reassessment. *JCL* 8, 541–64.

Vihman, M. 1981. Phonology and the development of the lexicon: Evidence from children's errors. *JCL* 8, 239–64.

Vihman, M., Macken, M., Miller, R., Simmons, H. and Miller, J. 1985. From babbling to speech: A re-assessment of the continuity issue. *Language* 61, 397–445.

de Villiers, J. and de Villiers, P 1973a. A cross-sectional study of the acquisition of grammatical morphemes in child speech. *Journal of Psycholinguistic Research* 2, 267–78.

—— 1973b. Development of the use of word order in comprehension. *Journal of Psycholinguistic Research* 2, 331–41.

—— 1974. Competence and performance in child language: Are children really competent to judge? *JCL* 1, 11–22.

de Villiers, P. and de Villiers, J. 1972. Early judgments of semantic and syntactic acceptability by children. *Journal of Psycholinguistic Research* 1, 299–310.

Volterra, V. and Taeschner, T. 1978. The acquisition and development of language by bilingual children. *JCL* 5, 311–26.

Vygotsky, L. 1962. *Thought and Language*. Cambridge, Mass.: MIT Press.

Wagner, K. 1985. How much do children say in a day? *JCL* 12, 475–87.

Wanner, E. and Gleitman, L. (eds) 1982. *Language Acquisition: The state of the art*. New York: Cambridge University Press.

Warden, D. 1981. Children's understanding of *ask* and *tell*. *JCL* 8, 139–49.

Webster, B., and Ingram, D. 1972. The comprehension and production of the anaphoric pronouns 'he, she, him, her' in normal and linguistically deviant children. *PRCLD* 4, 55–78.

Weeks, T. 1971. Speech registers in young children. *Child Development* 42, 1119–31.

Weir, R. 1962. *Language in the Crib*. The Hague: Mouton.

Wells, G. 1980. Adjustments in adult-child conversation: Some effects of interaction. In H. Giles, W. Robinson and P. Smith (eds), *Language: Social psychological perspectives*. Oxford: Pergamon Press.

—— 1982. Review of *Learning to Talk*, by J. McShane. *JCL* 9, 264–8.

—— 1985. *Language Development in the Preschool Years*. Cambridge: Cambridge University Press.

Wexler, K. and Cullicover, P. 1980. *Formal Principles of Language Acquisition*. Cambridge, Mass.: MIT Press.

Whitely, R. 1985. *The Intellectual and Social Organization of the Sciences*. New York: Clarendon Press.

Wickstrom, S., Goldstein, H. and Johnson, L. 1985. On the subject of subjects: Suggestions for describing subjects in language intervention studies. *JSHD* 50, 282–6.

Wilmer, H. 1970. Television: Technical and artistic aspects of videotape in psychiatric teaching. In M. Berger (ed.), *Videotape Techniques in Psychiatric Training and Treatment*. New York: Brunner/Mazel.

Winitz, H. 1959. Language skills of male and female kindergarten children. *JSHR* 2, 377–81.

Wittgenstein, L. 1954. *Philosophical Investigations*. Oxford: Basil Blackwell.

Wode, H. 1977. Four early stages in the development of L_1 acquisition. *JCL* 4, 87–102.

Wohlwill, J. 1973. *The Study of Behavioral Development*. New York: Academic Press.

Woods, A. Fletcher, P. and Hughes, A. 1986. *Statistics in Language Studies*. Cambridge: Cambridge University Press.

Wright, R. 1976. *Understanding Statistics: An informal introduction for the behavioral sciences*. New York: Harcourt, Brace, Jovanovich.

Yau, S. 1979. Natural word order in child language. *International Journal of Psycholinguistics* 6:2, 21–43.

Zimmerman, B. and Pike, E. 1972. Effects of modeling and reinforcement on the acquisition and generalization of question-asking behavior. *Child Development* 43, 892–907.

Index

age, 48–9
analysis, 77–97
  categories for, 77–82
  computers in, 89–92
  measurement in, 82–9
  statistical, 93–7
Atkinson, M., 20, 21, 98
autonomy (linguistic), 15–16

Barnes, S., Gutfreund, M., Satterly, D.
    and Wells, G., 4
behaviorism, 10, 13–14
Bloom, L., 26, 29, 33, 35–6, 93
  Bitetti Capatides, J. and Tackeff, J.,
    81–2, 99
  Lifter, K. and Broughton, J., 99
  Rocissano, L. and Hood, L., 37
  Tackeff, J. and Lahey, M., 16
Braunwald, S. and Breslin, R., 56–62; *see*
    also diary
Brown, R., 2, 9, 85–7

Child Language Data Exchange System
    (CHILDES), 37–8
Chomsky, C., 28–9
Chomsky, N., 7–10, 20, 76, 94
coding, 77–82
  a priori/post priori, 79–81
  category systems, 78–9
  nominal systems, 77–8
  parameters for, 79
  relationship to theory, 81–2
cognitivism (mentalism), 14–15
Crystal, D., 2–3, 85–7, 92

data collection, 67–70
  duration, 69–70
  frequency, 67–8
  innovations in, 69–70
  longevity, 70

data types, 26–7
  computerized, 37–8
  diaries, 55–62
  experimental, 29–31
  intuitions, 27–8
  tape (audio- and video-), 62–7
design, 67–9
  cross-sectional, 67
  experimental, 1, 2, 28–35
  longitudinal, 44, 67–8
  naturalistic, 2, 35–7
  time-lag, 68–9
development, 21, 48–9, 69, 85
  assumptions concerning, 69, 85
  relationship to age, 48–9
  theoretical requirement, 21
Developmental Sentence Scoring (DSA),
    51, 90
diary, 55–62
  advantages and assumptions, 55–6
  definition of diary study, 57
  disadvantages, 60–2
  format, 58–60

Eilers, R., Gavin, W. and Oller, D., 95
  Oller, D., Bull, D. and Gavin, W., 96
epistemology in CLR, 9–10
  behaviorist, 14
  scientific, 17–18
experimentation, 29–35, 123
  advantages, 31–2
  and comprehension, 33, 123
  problems in, 29–31
  replication, 32–3
  steps in, 34–5
  types, 33–4

Fassnacht, G., 36, 77–8, 83, 101
Furrow, D. and Nelson, K., 7

Furrow, D., Nelson, K. and Benedict,
　H., 3–4

generativism, 10, 15–17
Gleitman, L., Newport, E. and Gleitman,
　H., 4–6

infant speech perception, 95–7
interactionism, 15
interpretation, 97–101

Journal of Child Language, 2–3, 7
Jusczyk, P., Shea, S. and Aslin, R., 96–7

Language Assessment, Remediation, and
　Screening Procedure (LARSP), 92
LINGQUEST, 91
linguistics, 7–10, 17
　origins of CLR in, 8
　and psychology, 10
　as science, 9–10
　standard theory, 17
　theoretical influences on CLR, 7–8, 9

McKain, K., 95
Mahler, M., 72–4
mean length of utterance (MLU), 85–7
measurement, 82–97
　age/stage, 84–5
　criteria for acquisition, 88
　mean length of utterance (MLU), 85–7
　pragmatic and functional, 89
　purpose of, 82–4
　reliability of, 92–3
　statistical, 93–7
　type-token ratios, 87–8
methodology, 3, 16–17, 39–40, 101
　devaluation of, 101
　discussions in CLR literature, 3
　ethnomethodology, 39–40
　and standard theory, 16–17
models, 16; *see also* theory
motherese controversy, 3–7

Newport, E., Gleitman, H. and Gleitman,
　L., 3
number (N), 43–6, 94
　large, 45–6
　relationship to analysis, 94
　relationship to design, 46
　small, 43–5

observation/observers, 70–4

biases, 70–1
　setting and, 72–4
Ochs, E., 24, 37, 75–7
Oller, D. and Eilers, R., 95–6

practice of CLR (praxis), 1, 19, 103–11
　clusters in, 110–11
　in early 1970s, 104–6
　learning of, 1
　in mid-to-late 1970s, 106–7
　recent, 108–10
　relationship to theory, 19
　variables in, 103–4
pragmatics, 17, 89
psychology in CLR, 8–10

records, 37–8, 55–67
　audio and video, 62–7
　computerized, 37–8
　diary, 55–62
replication, 32–3

Systematic Analysis of Language
　Transcripts (SALT), 91
sample, 4, 42–6
　biases, 44
　heterogeneity vs homogeneity of, 4, 44,
　　46
　statistical influences on, 42
Schieffelin, B., 39–40
Schwartz, R., and Camarata, S., 6–7
setting, 73–4
statistics, 6–7, 93–7
　appropriateness in CLR, 94
　descriptive vs inferential, 93–4
　in infant speech perception, 95–7
　in motherese controversy, 6–7
　types in CLR, 97
Stern, W., 2, 29–30, 57–60
subjects, 41–51
　age of, 48–51
　biases in, 44
　function and selection of, 41–2
　gender of, 46–7
　number of, 42–6
　sibling position of, 47–8

theory, 7–8, 10–11, 13–17, 18, 19, 20–4
　development of, 19
　discussions in CLR literature, 7–8
　linguistic types in CLR, 15–17
　progressive and non-progressive,
　　18–19

psychological types in CLR, 13–15
reducing, 11
relationship to data, 22–4
relationship to method, 10
requirements of, 20–1
sketch (framework), 19
synthesizing, 11
transcription, 75–7; *see also* diary, format

unification of CLR, 8–9, 17–18, 54–5,
74, 102, 111
causes of disunity, 8–9, 17–18, 102

hindrances to, 54–5, 111
influences on, 74

variables: dependent and independent,
28–9, 33, 84, 86
videotaping, 62–7
advantages, 64–5
techniques, 65–7

Wells, C., 4, 51, 68, 69, 70–1, 78, 85,
88–9, 93, 97
Wohlwill, J., 48, 52, 67